# Set up Your Home Office

## Send Us Your Comments

To comment on this book or any other PRIMA TECH title, visit our reader response page on the Web at **www.prima-tech.com/comments**.

## How to Order

For information on quantity discounts, contact the publisher: Prima Publishing, P.O. Box 1260BK, Rocklin, CA 95677-1260; (916) 632-4400. On your letterhead, include information concerning the intended use of the books and the number of books you wish to purchase. For individual orders, turn to the back of this book for more information.

# Set up Your Home Office

## In a Weekend

**Faithe Wempen**

PRIMA TECH

A DIVISION OF PRIMA PUBLISHING

*To Margaret*

A Division of Prima Publishing

Prima Publishing and colophon are registered trademarks of Prima Communications, Inc. PRIMA TECH is a trademark of Prima Communications, Inc., Roseville, California 95661.

**Publisher:** Stacy L. Hiquet
**Marketing Manager:** Judi Taylor
**Associate Marketing Manager:** Jody Kennen
**Managing Editor:** Sandy Doell
**Acquisitions Editor:** Lynette Quinn
**Project Editor:** Melody Layne
**Copy Editor:** Kate Shoup Welsh
**Technical Reviewer:** Nancy Albright
**Proofreader:** Kim Benbow
**Interior Layout:** William Hartman
**Cover Design:** Prima Design Team
**Indexer:** Sherry Massey

ISBN: 0-7615-3054-1

Library of Congress Catalog Card Number: 0010664

Printed in the United States of America

00 01 02 03 04 BB 10 9 8 7 6 5 4 3 2 1

## ACKNOWLEDGMENTS

Thanks to all the Prima Tech editors for being so doggone nice to work for. It's a real pleasure to work with such flexible, good-natured people. The lead editors on this book were Lynette Quinn, who managed the early stages of the project by getting sales and management approval and handling contractual issues, and Melody Layne, who managed the chapter-by-chapter editorial process. Thanks to both for excellent work.

I also want to acknowledge Nancy Albright, who served as technical editor. When Prima asked me whom I wanted for my technical editor, Nancy was my immediate first choice. She has been running a successful home-based freelance business for longer than anyone I know (over 20 years), and gave generously of her expertise and ideas to this book.

## ABOUT THE AUTHOR

FAITHE WEMPEN is an A+ Certified computer technician and the owner of Your Computer Friend, a computer training and troubleshooting business in Indianapolis that provides beginners with one-on-one help with their PCs. She also holds an M.A. in English from Purdue University, where she taught English Composition and Business Writing. Her eclectic writing credits include not only computer books (40+ titles), software documentation, and training manuals, but also magazine articles, essays, fiction, and poetry.

# CONTENTS AT A GLANCE

# CONTENTS

# INTRODUCTION

Back in 1994, I was sitting in my cubicle in a big office, pushing paper and listening to the guy on the other side of the partition wall arguing with his mechanic on the phone, and I thought to myself, "This is *not* what I wanted to be when I grew up. What happened?"

That thought has probably occurred to a lot of people. As kids, we have these big dreams of the exciting careers we'll have, but somewhere along the way we allow people to convince us that we can't be anything we want. And before we know it, we find ourselves in the middle of a cubicle farm, collating memos and forwarding e-mail jokes.

But there's good news. We don't have to live and die in someone else's office. We can work for ourselves—from our own home offices—and make good money, too. There's a home-office revolution taking place in America right now, and almost anyone can be a part of it.

## Who Should Read This Book

This book is for the fed-up cubicle dweller with a product or service to sell who is ready to work from home. Although much of the advice in this book can also apply to a telecommuter, the book's primary slant is toward the self-employed entrepreneur.

I won't spend a lot of time helping you decide what product or service to sell because I figure you've probably given that a lot of thought already. If not, there are plenty of books on the market that specialize in helping you think through that decision.

People in the early planning-and-thinking stages can read this book to get an idea of what's involved in establishing a home office. But this book is primarily for the person who is ready to take some action. The person who is ready to turn that extra bedroom into an office. The person who is ready to have business cards printed. The person who is ready to start working in his or her bathrobe.

# How This Book is Organized

This book is based on a weekend format with chapters for each part of the weekend: Friday Evening, Saturday Morning, and so on. But those date and time designations are merely suggestions; you are free to read at your own pace and take as long as you need to for each step along the way.

- ✪ **Friday Night: The Work-at-Home Plan** helps you outline the rest of the weekend. You'll consider whether working from home is right for you (it isn't for everyone, by the way), whether you have enough space in your current residence to make it work, and whether you will need to hire any professional help, such as a lawyer or an accountant.

- ✪ **Saturday Morning: Setting Up Your Office Space** tells you more than you ever thought possible about the logistics of setting up an office in your home. You'll learn about business permits and zoning, choosing wall and floor coverings, planning for media jacks for phones and computer networks, and choosing furniture for comfort and ergonomics.

- **Saturday Afternoon: Selecting Computer Equipment** helps you pick the right electronics to equip your new office. You'll learn how to choose a computer system for various types of businesses, as well as peripherals, such as printers, scanners, and video equipment.

- **Saturday Evening: Your Connections to the World** helps you develop a plan for connecting with your clients, vendors, and other business associates. You'll select phone and fax services, choose a mailing address, and decide what type of Internet service is best for you.

- **Sunday Morning: Getting Business** addresses business startup concerns, such as developing a business plan and company policies, designing business cards and stationery, and planning your advertising and marketing strategies.

- **Sunday Afternoon: Finances and Recordkeeping** provides a basic tutorial on business banking and financial records. You'll learn about the different types of business bank accounts available, how to handle your business's accounting, how to plan for taxes, what insurance you need, and whether to incorporate. You'll also learn about the pros and cons of accepting credit cards and how to set up a retirement plan for yourself.

In addition, the book contains some appendixes that offer specialized information:

- **Appendix A: Home Office Resources Online** points you to dozens of helpful Web sites on the Internet with vital information for the home worker.

- **Appendix B: A Concise Guide to Schedule C** walks you line by line through one of the most intimidating parts of filing business taxes: filling out *Schedule C, Profit or Loss from Business.*

# Conventions

Several special elements in this book will help you on your way!

**TIP**

Tips offer insider information about a technology, a company, or a technique.

**NOTE**

Notes provide background information and insight into why things work the way they do.

**CAUTION**

Cautions warn you of possible hazards and point out pitfalls that typically plague beginners.

# Talk Back!

I'd like to hear about your experiences in using this book to set up your home office. Was the advice in the book helpful? Were there any areas where your experience did not match what was described? Were you looking for information about an aspect of home office life that you didn't find here? Write to me at faithe@wempen.com.

By the way, if you liked the book, you can help keep it in print by making your opinion known. Swing on over to http://www.amazon.com and http://www.BarnesandNoble.com and post a review of the book that others can read who are looking for a home office book. It costs nothing and provides a service to others as well.

# The Work-at-Home Plan

- ✿ Why Work at Home?
- ✿ Telecommuting versus Your Own Business
- ✿ Establishing Your Plan
- ✿ Avoiding Common Pitfalls
- ✿ Can You Do It All Yourself?

**W**ork in your bathrobe and make big bucks! Set your own hours! Be your own boss!

Those infomercials make it sound pretty good, don't they? And the amazing thing is, those statements about working at home are more or less accurate. I've been working at home since 1995 when I quit my middle-management job at a publishing house, and I *do* work in my bathrobe. I *do* set my own hours. I *am* my own boss. And the first year out of the rat race, I doubled my income.

But there's more to working at home than just these luxurious, highly-touted perks. Those infomercials don't tell you that you'll be working in your bathrobe because you've been up for 35 hours straight working on a project with a tight deadline, or that being your own boss means you have to deny yourself that new computer system because it's not in the company budget.

There's plenty to think about when planning a home office, and I get into all those nitty-gritty details in later chapters. But in this session, I just want you to start thinking about working from home in a general way to make sure that you're making the right decision before pouring a lot of time and money into setting up your workspace.

# Why Work at Home?

I *love* working at home, and I can't imagine ever going back to the 9-to-5 office world. I don't even have any business clothes anymore, and I'm sure an employer wouldn't like me to show up in my current company uniform (that is, shorts and a t-shirt in summer, sweatpants and a t-shirt in winter).

Some of my favorite things about being self-employed and working from home are

- **No set hours.** You decide when you'll start and finish, what days you'll take your vacation, and what weekends you'll work. Want to take the afternoon off and sleep in the sun? There's nobody to tell you not to.

- **No distractions**. There's no chatty officemate telling you about his family, and no staff meetings to take you away from important projects. There's also no middle management and nobody else's unwashed coffee cup in the sink.

- **You work independently.** With most work-at-home jobs (telecommuting excluded), you're judged on your own output and productivity. Someone else's failure is not your problem. When I was working in an office, if one of my co-workers dropped the ball, I was often asked to help fix the problem—in addition to doing my own work. As a freelancer, if I fix a problem that someone else caused, I get paid for it.

- **Your office space is your own**. There are no corporate policies for what you can or can't do with your office space. The arrangement, equipment, and even standards of cleanliness and clutter are all up to your own judgment.

- **You decide the course of your career**. If you get bored doing one thing, you can do something else. When you're self-employed you can continually reinvent yourself by taking classes, getting certifications, or simply pursuing different business. When I started out, for example, I was primarily a book editor. I branched out from

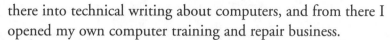

there into technical writing about computers, and from there I opened my own computer training and repair business.

- **You choose the projects**. You don't have to do anything you don't want to. If a certain project doesn't sound appealing, you can turn it down politely with no hard feelings. Just try that at a regular job!

- **No long-term commitment**. You aren't stuck with a bad boss or a disagreeable task indefinitely. If you don't like a particular project you're working on, it'll be over soon and you can choose more wisely the next time.

- **No supervision**. You, and only you, are responsible for the quality and timeliness of your work. Nobody can tell you how or when to work on it. As long as the work gets done, your clients will usually not care how that occurred.

- **Taxes**. As a home-worker, you can deduct a portion of your mortgage or rent payment, plus a portion of your utilities and other household expenses, from your federal income tax. You can also deduct part of your health insurance payments, your business-related office expenses, and many other items that people who work in offices can't.

Sounds pretty good, right? But I have many friends who have tried working at home and have given it up to go back to the corporate world after six months to a year. When I ask them why, they give some very valid reasons:

- **No set hours.** Most people think they will work fewer hours when working from home, but the opposite often turns out to be true. With no separation between home and work, you might find that work is sucking up too much time, and you actually have less time for family and home than before.

- **No distractions**. If you're a naturally social person, being by yourself all day can be lonely and depressing. Being somewhat of a solitary type, I have never experienced this personally, but my more gregarious friends assure me that it's the single biggest factor in their returning to office life. There is also little to distract you from working all the time, including right through your lunch hour and your son's soccer game. Believe it or not, overworking is a much more serious problem than underworking for self-employed people.

✪ **You work independently.** For most work-at-homers, there are few opportunities for teamwork and cooperation with others. You do your work alone, often with little feedback. Without getting regular feedback and objective analysis of your work, it's easy to allow your motivation and quality to slip. You don't know what you're doing wrong or right, so you have to be your own cheerleader and critic.

✪ **Your office space is your own**. You must somehow find space in your already crowded home for a desk, a chair, and whatever else you need to do your job. You might even need to rewire a room to get the needed electrical outlets. Then you need to furnish that space, and the cost for every last pencil comes out of your own pocket.

✪ **You decide the course of your career**. Without corporate backing, you must pay for any training or professional development yourself. And while you're off at training, you aren't earning any money—there's no such thing as paid time off for the self-employed. Consequently, many self-employed people don't get the training they need to stay competitive, and their skills become dated.

✪ **You choose the work**. That means you have to *find* the work, and convince others that you're the best person for the job. Not only do you need to be an expert at what you do, but you also have to be a sales and marketing whiz. Self-employment means wearing many hats, not all of which are a good fit.

✪ **No long-term commitment**. You sometimes won't know where your next dollar is coming from. There are no regular paychecks. And if an important client is slow to pay, you might have trouble making the mortgage payment. There's no parent company with a vested interest in your success and no company-paid insurance or benefits.

- **No supervision**. You've got more than enough rope to hang your-self. With nobody leaning over your shoulder to see that you get the work done, you might be tempted to take too many afternoons off and fail to get the work done. Then you'll start losing clients and be caught in a no-win downward spiral.

- **Taxes**. If you're self-employed, you must pay self-employment tax, which can more than offset any tax benefits of a home-office deduction. In addition, there are some tax complications when you sell a home that you've been using for a home-office tax deduction. (I'll talk more about those in the section titled "Tax Planning" on Sunday afternoon.) You are also responsible for making quarterly estimated tax payments, and if you're not careful to set aside enough money, you can get into some serious IRS debt.

Did you notice that every single one of my pros was somebody else's con?

The bottom line: Working from home, and especially working for your-self, is very different from working in an office. If it fits your personali-ty and strengths, it can be heaven on Earth. If it doesn't, it can be…well, *not* heaven.

# Telecommuting versus Your Own Business

Not everyone with a home office is self-employed; telecommuting is a very popular alternative. A telecommuter works from home, but remains a full- or part-time employee of a larger company, usually with a salary and benefits. Telecommuting has many of the benefits of home employ-ment, such as the ability to dress down every day, but also some of the security of a regular office job, such as a regular, reliable paycheck.

More and more companies are allowing workers to telecommute these days, because it can be a win-win situation for everyone involved. Employees are happy because they have fewer interruptions, more free-dom, and are less likely to look for new jobs anytime soon. Employers are happy because they don't have to rent extra office space to house the telecommuting employees.

If you're telecommuting, your company might be willing to pay for some of the expenses involved in setting up your home office, such as buying furniture and equipment, paying for phone, fax, and Internet setup, and so on. It doesn't hurt to ask.

**NOTE** In my years of freelancing, I have had several happy clients try to coax me into a telecommuting relationship with them. For me, it wasn't an attractive proposition because I like the variety of working for different clients. But your situation might be different, so don't be too quick to dismiss these offers if they come along.

There are also different flavors of telecommuting. Some companies want you to work just as if your home office were a remote location of the company. They want you to keep regular office hours, answer the phone with the company name, and maybe even come to headquarters one day a week for meetings. Other arrangements are looser. Other companies are more interested in your results than your methods and will let you decide when and how to get your work done.

## It Isn't for Everyone...

I'm always surprised when I talk to someone who worked from home for a while but didn't like it. But believe it or not, there are a lot of people for whom it just isn't a good fit. I outlined some of the potential drawbacks earlier in the chapter. It all depends on your personality, work habits, and preferences.

Working at home might not be right for you if

○ **You are an outgoing, gregarious person who makes friends easily at work**. If so, you will probably be lonely and bored at home (unless your home business involves meeting the public daily).

- **You work best when someone sets a schedule for you and checks on you frequently**. If so, you might have difficulty setting your own schedule and following it without any prompting.

- **You get sidetracked easily**. If so, you might not be very productive at home where there's nobody to tell you not to spend three hours watching daytime TV.

- **You can focus on only one task at a time**. If so, you might not be able to manage working for several clients at once out of your small office space at home.

- **You're a big-picture, creative thinker with no patience for details**. If so, you'll hate the fact that in your office, not only are you the idea generator, but also the idea implementer (as well as the typist, the receptionist, and the trashcan-emptier).

- **You're a sloppy record-keeper**. If so, you'll find it difficult to maintain the accurate business records needed to keep you on the right side of tax law.

In short, the ideal at-home worker is somewhat of a loner, very independent, self-motivated, a logical thinker, detail-oriented, capable of multi-tasking, and a careful record keeper. Is that you? Use Worksheet 1.1 to make a preliminary evaluation.

By the way, none of these are deal-breakers; if you see yourself in one or more of them, that doesn't mean you should immediately abandon all plans to work at home. However, keep them in mind, because lack of the right work-at-home personality is the number-one reason why home businesses don't last.

For each line, mark the column that describes how you would rate each aspect of working at home.

Did you mark mostly positives? Then your personality is probably a good fit for working at home. Did you mark more neutrals or negatives? Well, I don't want to discourage you from pursuing your dream, but be aware that you are not the typical home-worker type, and try to construct your

## Worksheet 1.1  Is Working at Home Right for Me?

| Condition | Positive | Neutral | Negative |
|---|---|---|---|
| There are no fixed office hours to separate home time from work time. | | | |
| There are no co-workers to socialize with. | | | |
| You meet deadlines and satisfy customers without any assistance from others in most cases. | | | |
| There are no group projects or team efforts. | | | |
| You are responsible for defining and equipping your office space. | | | |
| Projects are typically of short duration with very little routine. | | | |
| You wear many hats, from salesperson to mail clerk. | | | |
| There is no supervision, and very little feedback of any kind. | | | |
| You choose and pay for any continuing education or training that will benefit your career. | | | |
| Total from each column: | | | |

work experience so that it provides what you need to be satisfied. If you're a very social person, for example, maybe you can spend a few days a week visiting clients or having lunch with friends to relieve the isolation. You get the idea.

# Take a Break

So what do you think? Is working from home right for you? Take a few minutes away from this book, and chat with some friends and relations about the possibility. It's always helpful to get other people's opinions. If your spouse starts laughing hysterically when you bring up the prospect of working unsupervised for hours on end, perhaps it's a sign you should reconsider.

# Establishing Your Plan

The purpose of this weekend project is to turn your home office dream into a reality. I'll be taking you step-by-step through each of the decisions and considerations required to set up an office, both in terms of buying stuff and in making plans to keep the business running smoothly.

You don't need to make any big decisions tonight, but I want you to start thinking about the big questions in a general way. Then, starting tomorrow morning, I'll help you work out the details.

## Where Will You Locate Your Office?

Nothing else can proceed until you make this decision. Will you put your office in a spare room by itself or set up business in a desk in the corner of your dining room? Or will you remodel a part of your house to create the space? I'll get into the nitty-gritty of space requirements in tomorrow morning's session.

## What Equipment Will You Need?

Equipment is a big topic. Later in the weekend I'll help you pick out computer equipment, telephones, copiers, and other electronics, as well as office furniture. But for the moment, make a quick list of the general categories of equipment you'll need to make a go of it. You can make your final decisions later, but you should at least begin thinking about the following:

- ✿ **Furniture.** Do you need a desk and chair? Probably. What about another chair or a waiting area for visitors? A worktable or conference area in addition to your desk where several people can work together if needed?

- ✿ **Storage.** Will you need a bookcase? A file cabinet? Some storage drawers? Or maybe a whole separate closet to store things?

- ✿ **Lighting.** If you're not relying on an overhead light in the room, what kind of light fixtures will you need? Table lamps? Wall-mounted lights?

- ✿ **Computers.** Will you need a computer? And if so, will it be a PC or a Mac? Should it be a desktop unit or a portable?

- ✿ **Computer input and output.** Will you need a printer for your computer? How about a scanner? A digital camera? A modem?

- ✿ **Decorations.** How much do you plan to spend, if anything, on making the office look attractive?

**CAUTION**

◆ ◆ ◆ ◆ ◆ ◆ ◆ ◆ ◆ ◆ ◆ ◆ ◆ ◆ ◆ ◆ ◆ ◆ ◆ ◆ ◆ ◆ ◆ ◆ ◆ ◆ ◆ ◆ ◆ ◆ ◆ ◆ ◆ ◆ ◆ ◆ ◆ ◆

When dreaming about your ideal office, it's easy to get carried away and convince yourself that you really need certain luxuries that won't affect your business profitability. True, whatever you buy for the business will be tax-deductible, but if you don't need an item, it's seldom a good deal.

◆ ◆ ◆ ◆ ◆ ◆ ◆ ◆ ◆ ◆ ◆ ◆ ◆ ◆ ◆ ◆ ◆ ◆ ◆ ◆ ◆ ◆ ◆ ◆ ◆ ◆ ◆ ◆ ◆ ◆ ◆ ◆ ◆ ◆ ◆ ◆ ◆ ◆

# What's Your Budget?

Like it or not, you'll probably need to limit what you spend to set up your home office. If you plan to telecommute, your employer might pick up the tab, but even then there's likely to be a limit.

So how much should you plan on spending? That depends on several factors, the first of which is the type of business and its requirements. Some businesses don't require anything special at all—perhaps a desk, a chair, and a pad of paper. Others require computers, software, storage facilities…well, you get the idea.

"Okay," you're probably thinking, "at least give me a ballpark estimate." Table 1.1 shows a range of prices for some common items, and I'll help you find the best values and select specific models later in the weekend.

## TABLE 1.1  PRICE RANGES FOR BIG-TICKET HOME OFFICE ITEMS

| Item | Cheapest | Mid-Range | Most Expensive |
|---|---|---|---|
| Desk | $100 | $200 | $1,000+ |
| Chair | $100 | $200 | $900 |
| File Cabinet | $60 | $100 | $500+ |
| Computer | $500 | $2000 | $5000 |
| Printer | $75 | $200 | $2000+ |
| Bookshelf | $100 | $200 | $1000+ |
| Phone | $20 | $60 | $250 |
| Fax Machine | $100 | $200 | $600 |
| Copier | $200 | $600 | $3000+ |

As you can tell from this table, the prices for common office items vary tremendously. You can buy some version of an item for just about whatever you have to spend. That's why careful shopping is so important, as I'll discuss in the Saturday morning session.

## How Will You Connect to the World?

Take a moment to consider how you will communicate with your employer or your customers. Will you use e-mail? Telephone? Overnight delivery? Or a combination of all these, plus other ways?

To be successful, you'll need to set up the communication channels for your business in advance. That might mean any or all of the following:

- Getting a post-office box
- Setting up an overnight delivery account (FedEx, UPS, and so on)
- Establishing an account with a local courier service for same-day local deliveries
- Installing a second telephone line
- Buying a fax machine and perhaps getting a separate phone line for it as well
- Getting a separate e-mail account for business
- Setting up high-speed Internet access in your office area

Not all these items might be feasible, given your budget, or even necessary. Pick the one or two methods of communication you think you will use the most, and focus your attention and budget on them first. For example, if you think you will get a lot of orders faxed to you, get a fax machine with its own phone line, and then worry later about your Internet connectivity. I'll explain these choices in a lot more detail later in the Saturday evening session.

Use Worksheet 1.2 to jot down any thoughts you've had about the physical location and equipment of your future office.

## Worksheet 1.2 The Physical Plan

| Topic | Key Decisions | Notes |
|---|---|---|
| Location | Separate room? Which room? Remodeling needed? | |
| Furniture | What items needed? Do you have any of them already? | |
| Storage | What do you need to store? Where might you store it? | |
| Lighting | Do you need an overhead light? | |
| Computer | Do you need one? PC or Mac? | |
| Decorating | Would decorating the office help your business? If so, how? | |
| Budget | About how much do you have to spend? Can this amount change if you later decide you need to do more? | |
| Internet | Do you need an Internet connection for business? Will a regular one be okay, or should it be a high-speed connection? Do you need a separate business e-mail address? | |
| Mail | Do you need a post-office box? If not, where will mail for the business be delivered? | |
| Telephone | Do you need a separate business phone line? If not, how will you handle incoming business calls on your personal line? | |
| Fax | Do you need to be able to send and receive faxes? | |

Your answers here are by no means the last word on these subjects. I'll give you a lot more information on each of them later in the book, and that information might change your decisions. But it's important that you begin roughly sketching the outlines of your business mentally so you have a big-picture perspective on it right from the start.

# How Will You Get and Keep Customers?

Remember, the whole point of being in business is to make a profit so you can support yourself. All the expenses you incur in setting up your home office must eventually be offset by the profit you make.

If you're telecommuting, getting customers is not an issue for you—your employer is your customer. Your employer is probably your only customer, too. Many employers frown upon moonlighting, especially if you're using the equipment they have paid for to get you set up at home.

For those of you working for yourselves, however, getting and keeping customers is a primary concern.

## Getting Customers

First and foremost, where will your customers come from? The answer, of course, depends on the type of business you do. If you're offering a service, your customers will come from a local area. If you're selling a product, you could potentially have customers all over the world, especially with the help of the Internet.

To get customers, you must make people aware of your product or service and give them a reason to want it. All salesmanship boils down to those two things.

Here are some of the most common ways to get people's attention and convince them that they need what you have to sell:

✿ **Word of mouth.** One satisfied customer tells someone, and they tell someone, and so on.

✿ **Broadcast advertising.** Placing ads on radio and TV can be expensive, but might be worth it in certain industries.

✿ **Print advertising.** Advertising in newspapers, magazines, and direct mailings is a great way to distribute coupons and other specials. You can also deliver flyers yourself house to house.

✿ **Internet advertising.** Promoting your business online can be very inexpensive compared to other advertising methods and, depending on what you're selling, can be very effective.

✿ **Direct sales calls.** Do you have the chutzpah to call potential customers on the phone or visit them in person? Direct sales is a very tough road to go down, but it can be profitable if you are persistent and thick-skinned.

✿ **Networking**. I have gotten more work from referrals from fellow freelancers than from any other source. If you get to know others who are in your line of work and cultivate friendly relationships with them, they will often send clients your way when their own schedules are too full.

✿ **Directories**. Depending on your profession, there might be one or more professional directories published that you can be a part of, either for free or for a small fee. There might also be directories on the Internet in which you can participate.

I'll go into salesmanship and marketing in more detail on Sunday morning.

## Keeping Customers

Repeat patronage is the key to almost any business. If a customer is happy with the buying experience, he or she will be back. If not, someone else's business will benefit instead.

Maintaining your business means building your good reputation, both with each individual customer and with the buying community as a whole. Marketing can help build a reputation, and I'll talk about that on Sunday morning, but even more important is the experience you provide to each individual customer. They say that the average happy customer tells one or two people about his or her experience, but that the average dissatisfied customer tells eight people. That means it's much easier to get a bad reputation than a good one through customer word of mouth. To combat that potential for downward spiral, you must make sure that every customer (or at least almost every one) is satisfied.

So how do you satisfy customers? You give them, at the minimum, what they expect. Ideally, you want to give them more than they expect, to delight them. If your deadline is Tuesday, get the job done on Monday. If you have time, deliver an order personally instead of calling the customer to come pick it up. There are all kinds of little ways to keep your customers coming back. On Sunday morning, you'll develop a business plan and a written statement of your work ethic—including how you'll treat your customers. I'll provide some specific activities that have been successful for me in the section "Establishing Your Work Ethic" on Sunday morning. But if you just approach each customer's business with the aim to provide more, you won't have any trouble rising to the top of your profession.

Use Worksheet 1.3 to record your initial ideas about getting and keeping customers. Don't worry if you don't have any thoughts yet on a certain topic; just leave it blank and you'll work on it some more later in the book.

## How Will You Record Your Finances?

Precise financial record keeping is important for several reasons, but the biggest one is to satisfy the IRS. As a business owner, you're responsible for paying taxes, and you had better have all the numbers accounted for in the event of an audit.

**Worksheet 1.3  Customers**

| Topic | Key Decisions | Notes |
|---|---|---|
| Physical location of customers | Will your customers be mostly local? State-wide? Nationwide? International? | |
| Sales targeting | Will your customers be from the general public, or a specific market segment? | |
| Awareness | How will you make potential customers aware of your product or service? | |
| Incentive | How will you make your product or service attractive to buy? | |
| Repeat business | What will you do to make sure the customers are happy? | |

I'll explain more about record keeping in Sunday afternoon's session, devoted entirely to finances, but for now I want you to think about how you will handle your accounting. If your business is a one-person operation, you might not need an accountant, except perhaps at tax time. Just keep good records of each purchase for the business (and save all receipts), and save copies of the invoices you create for each client. The key is to document every penny of income and outflow. If you took a bookkeeping or accounting class in school, you probably have enough know-how to set up a simple record-keeping system.

**TIP** If you don't know anything about accounting, consider hiring an accountant to set up a system for you that you can run yourself on an everyday basis. That way you can have a professional-quality accounting system without having to pay for a full-time accountant.

Many owners of small businesses have had good luck using computer software for accounting. PeachTree Complete and QuickBooks are two popular programs in that category. I have a friend who teaches classes in PeachTree Complete, and she swears it is the superior accounting program, but I have found it difficult to learn. In contrast, I took to Quick-Books immediately, and that's the program I use for my own accounting.

Although it's more expensive, some people prefer to have an accountant or a bookkeeper help them on a daily or weekly basis. I'll talk more about using professional services later in this session.

Use Worksheet 1.4 to record your first impressions about how to handle the business accounting. As with the other quiz decisions you've recorded, these might change later, and that's okay.

## Avoiding Common Pitfalls

Now that you have your general plan, you're practically ready to start your business! So what could go wrong? Plenty. Lots of home-based businesses fail, and it's not always just a question of being unable to make money. Here are some of the most dangerous business-killing dragons. Each of these are discussed in more detail later in the book, but I want you to start thinking about them now in a general way:

✪ **Procrastination.** In other words, putting off until tomorrow what you don't feel like doing today. See "Avoiding Procrastination" in the Sunday morning session for some tips on disciplining yourself to work.

---

### Worksheet 1.4  Accounting

| Key Decisions | Notes |
|---|---|
| Would you be comfortable using a computer program to manage the business finances? | |
| Do you think you'll want an accountant to set up your accounting system initially for you? | |
| Is it worth it to you to pay an accountant or bookkeeper to handle all the day-to-day inflows and outflows? | |
| Will you want help preparing your federal income taxes, or will you handle them yourself with a tax-preparation computer program? | |

---

✿ **Distractions.** The people, places, and things that keep you from getting your work done. See "Derailing Distractions" on Sunday morning to eliminate distractions from your workday.

✿ **Poor ergonomics.** *Ergonomics* refers to the proper positioning of your tables, chairs, computers, and other equipment to avoid bodily stress or injury. Check out "Understanding Ergonomics" in the Saturday morning session for the full scoop.

✿ **Sloppy record keeping.** Remember, you're responsible for keeping good business records. Letting your receipts and invoices pile up can spell financial ruin for your business. See the Sunday afternoon session for details.

✿ **Failure to pay taxes.** As a self-employed person, you're responsible for withholding enough of your income to pay quarterly tax payments. If you don't, all kinds of horrible things can happen, up to and including bankruptcy. The section "Tax Planning" on Sunday afternoon should help you get a grip on your tax responsibilities.

# Can You Do It All Yourself?

As you've seen so far in this chapter, self-employment often means wearing many different hats, from accountant to janitor to no-nonsense supervisor, and paying attention to things that you might never have needed to worry about before, such as filing estimated taxes and planning a marketing strategy. Is all of this starting to feel a little daunting? Well, it need not, because *you don't have to do everything yourself.* If you have enough income to offset the expense, you can hire professionals in various areas to handle those parts of the business that you don't feel confident about.

## Accountant

An accountant can help you set up your bookkeeping system, either on paper or in a computer program such as QuickBooks. He or she can also help you determine how much you need to pay on a quarterly basis for your estimated taxes and can prepare your federal and state taxes at year-end.

## Bookkeeper

A bookkeeper is like an accountant, but less expensive. Bookkeepers typically are not trained to evaluate financial situations and make recommendations; they're more concerned with financial record keeping. A bookkeeper can implement the system that your accountant sets up for you, recording each income and expense item and providing a tidy record from which your accountant can work at tax time.

## Legal Services

If you plan to set up a corporation, or use contracts in your business, consider getting help from a lawyer. Although their services are rather expensive per hour, their work can more than pay for itself in the long run through better-written contractual agreements and lack of hassling with improperly worded corporate documents.

## Computer Consultant

A computer consultant can set up your computer equipment, install the software, and make sure everything works together. Then, later, if you need it, a consultant can provide software training and problem troubleshooting.

**NOTE**  If you're handy with a computer, you can probably do most of the PC troubleshooting yourself. Buy a copy of my book **Tune Up Your PC In a Weekend**, also published by Prima Tech, which will tell you what you need to know about troubleshooting Windows 98 systems.

## Web Designers

If you have decided that your business needs a Web site, you can create one yourself using just about any word processor. However, it might not be professional looking or convey the look and feel you want, and it might not be capable of handling online ordering and other operations you want. On the other hand, if you hire a professional Web designer to create and manage your Web site, you can have all the whiz-bang features that the big boys have, without having to learn Web programming yourself.

Many people are disappointed by their online sales. They spend thousands of dollars on a fancy Web site with online ordering, only to find that their online sales are less than a few hundred dollars a month. Check out your competition first, and see whether anyone else who sells your particular product or service is making money online.

## Advertising and Marketing Agencies

If your business's initial success will depend heavily on getting new customers, you might want to turn over your advertising or marketing to a professional who can design a campaign to sell your products and services to your intended audience. Be aware, however, that such services aren't cheap. Consider carefully whether such a big investment will pay off in increased profits. You might want to start small, with advertising that you devise yourself, and gradually build up to using a professional service when you have the revenue to justify it.

## Moving On...

By now your head is probably swimming with ideas for office logistics, for advertising and marketing, and for the money and professional accolades you'll get in your new career. That's great! So sleep on those ideas, and tomorrow morning you'll start tackling all the nitty-gritty details.

# Setting Up Your Office Space

Remember when you were in grade school how exciting it was the first day of each school year? You'd arrive at school to find your new desk, and you'd place your brand-new pencils, notepads, paste, and crayons carefully in the drawer, full of expectation. Setting up your office for your new, exciting career at home can be just as much fun, and just as full of hopeful expectation. In this session, I'll help you choose the office space and furniture that will form the core part of your new workspace.

## Is It Legal?

Before you shell out a lot of money equipping your new workspace, check your local zoning ordinances. In some areas (particularly upscale suburbs), it's illegal to use your home for business purposes. Some ordinances prevent only businesses with certain characteristics that tend to bring down property values—for example, an auto-repair business that leaves many cars parked in a yard or a dentist office whose clients' comings and goings dramatically increase the traffic on a quiet street. However, other ordinances do not distinguish one business from another. Sure, you could quietly violate your local ordinance and nobody would probably be the wiser, but if you got caught, the penalty might be a stiff fine and the closure of your business. It's best to stay on the right side of the law at all times.

In some areas, home businesses are permitted as long as you take out a business license (which usually involves paying an annual registration fee). Other areas require a use permit, which is similar to a license but focused primarily on a business that uses a residential location.

So what's the case in your neighborhood? First you need to find out whom to ask. If you're in a city, start with the local government. If there is no Building Inspector, Zoning Administration, or Planning Department, the mayor's office might be a good place to start. That won't be the right place to ask, but whoever answers the phone there will direct you to the correct office. If you're not in a city, try your county sheriff's office. Then once you get hold of the right office, ask the following two questions:

- How is my property zoned?
- What is allowed in my zone?

## How Is My Property Zoned?

Zoning ordinances typically place a property into one of four classifications:

- Residential
- Commercial
- Industrial
- Agricultural

Residential is further divided into single-family units and multiple-family units. If you are zoned as agricultural, you should have no problems operating a home business. If you are zoned as commercial, there should be no problem there either. But you're probably in a residential zone, and that's where the restrictions and regulations kick in.

# What Is Allowed in My Zone?

Most communities have some sort of ordinance that prevents businesses from operating in residential zones. That's for your own property-value protection—it's not a bad thing. It keeps a convenience store from springing up in the lot next door to you, after all.

Usually the zoning regulations distinguish between a business and a profession and allow people to practice their professions from home. The allowed professions list might include artists, musicians, doctors, lawyers, and psychologists. Depending on the area, it might also include barber and beauty shops, real-estate agencies, music and dance instruction, and building contracting.

Further regulations might be in effect that are designed to keep your home business from acting too much like a commerce-drawing facility. You might be prohibited from using your street address in advertisements, hanging a sign in your yard for the business, or using an outside building, such as a garage, in which to do business. Most of these regulations are designed to make your business as invisible as possible from the street, thereby maintaining residential property values.

Most areas have a court or board that you can appeal to for a zoning variance. In your appeal, you can explain why the current zoning restriction in your area should not apply to you, giving specific reasons. If the court or board agrees, they grant you an exemption.

If you violate a zoning ordinance, and someone in authority finds out about it, you'll receive a written notice ordering you to stop. There might be a fine associated too, either initially or after a certain number of days if you refuse to stop. If you continue to operate in violation of the ordinance, the court might get an injunction or a court order prohibiting you from doing business. From there, you hire a lawyer and go to court to defend yourself. If you violate an injunction, you could potentially go to jail.

**TIP**  Unh neighbors turn in most of the people who are caught violating zoning ordinances. Try to maintain friendly relations with your neighbors for this reason, and encourage neighbors to come to you with any concerns or complaints. It's much easier to resolve an issue privately than to deal with a zoning board or court.

If you live in a neighborhood with an association, such as a planned community or condo, there might be additional rules to consider. Some communities have a rule about how many cars a resident can have parked on the street, for example. So if you think you will frequently have more customers at your house than can park in your driveway at once, you might consider arranging additional parking. Perhaps you can create more parking spaces behind the house, or pay a neighbor a small monthly fee to use his or her driveway occasionally.

# Choosing Your Office Space

The next step is to identify the part of your home that will function as the office. This is a biggie! Spend some time carefully considering all your options.

## Space Requirements

First, decide on the amount of space required. The amount of space you need depends almost entirely on what you plan to do for a living in that home office. Someone who's doing quilting and weaving, for example, will need something completely different from someone who is buying and selling collectibles, and someone who is working primarily with a computer all day will have different needs still.

For a job that involves sitting down most of the time at a desk, a 10×10-foot spare bedroom usually works well. If you need to keep an inventory, the bedroom's closet can suffice, or you might need to put overflow into

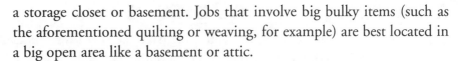

a storage closet or basement. Jobs that involve big bulky items (such as the aforementioned quilting or weaving, for example) are best located in a big open area like a basement or attic.

Think also of the space you will need for office equipment. If you need a full-sized copier, count on it taking up at least a 2-foot square area. If you need a computer and printer, that will occupy most of a 2×3-foot desk. It all adds up quickly to claim your workspace.

Finally, think of your storage needs—not just inventory, but the items you need to keep an office running. In my office, for example, I've got two big file cabinets with client records, a cabinet for office supplies (pens, tape, extra printer toner, copy paper, and so on), and a bookshelf with professional reference materials. Suddenly that 10×10-foot space isn't looking so large anymore, is it?

What if you don't even have a 10×10-foot space? Well, you might not need a completely separate room for your business, depending, of course, on what you'll be doing. Some people, such as writers and editors, for example, need only enough space to set up a computer. That could be a small desk in one corner of any room in the house.

**CAUTION**

◆ ◆ ◆ ◆ ◆ ◆ ◆ ◆ ◆ ◆ ◆ ◆ ◆ ◆ ◆ ◆ ◆ ◆ ◆ ◆ ◆ ◆ ◆ ◆ ◆ ◆ ◆ ◆ ◆ ◆ ◆ ◆ ◆ ◆ ◆ ◆ ◆ ◆ ◆

You might not be able to take a home-office deduction on your federal taxes if the space for your office is not a well-defined area such as a room. Check with an accountant for the latest regulations.

◆ ◆ ◆ ◆ ◆ ◆ ◆ ◆ ◆ ◆ ◆ ◆ ◆ ◆ ◆ ◆ ◆ ◆ ◆ ◆ ◆ ◆ ◆ ◆ ◆ ◆ ◆ ◆ ◆ ◆ ◆ ◆ ◆ ◆ ◆ ◆ ◆ ◆ ◆

Even if you don't have a separate room for the office, I strongly encourage you to have a desk that's exclusively for business use. For one thing, it helps keep all the paperwork and paraphernalia confined to a defined area, where you can find things easily when you're in a hurry. There's also a psychological benefit: When you sit down at your desk, you're "at work," and less focused on the distractions of the household around you.

# Remodeling to Create Office Space

If you decide that you don't have the space for the kind of office you'll need, you have the following options:

- Abandon the idea of working from home (not the most attractive option).

- Plan to rent office space somewhere nearby (which cancels out many of the work-at-home benefits, although you'll still be working for yourself).

- Remodel your home so that you can have an office.

Of course, remodeling is a time-, labor-, and money-intensive project that shouldn't be undertaken lightly. But if you have the budget for it, you might consider adding on a room especially for your home office or converting an unused space into a usable area. Attics, basements, garage workshops, sun porches, storage closets, and utility rooms are all prime candidates for remodeling. You might even build a separate building on your property if your local building codes permit it and if you have the money.

When designing a home office space, make sure that

- **There are enough electrical outlets**. By enough, I mean at least one two-plug outlet on every wall, possibly more, and every one of them a three-prong, grounded outlet. In addition, if you plan to use high-powered equipment, such as a large copier, consider putting your office on a separate electrical circuit.

- **The floor covering is easy to maintain**. In an office, there's typically a lot of equipment piled in, which makes it hard to run a vacuum on carpeting. Consider tile or linoleum flooring.

- **The lighting is adequate for your task**. Consider installing an overhead light fixture with a rheostat for adjusting the light level. A ceiling fan might be useful too, depending on your home's heating/cooling efficiency.

✿ **The room is heated/cooled adequately**. If you're converting an attic, basement, or garage, check that the insulation and heating system is adequate to make you comfortable in the room year-round. You might need to put in a separate baseboard heater from the rest of the house and an air conditioner.

Get some help with the plans; hire an architect to prepare the plans and specifications, making sure they follow local health, safety, and building regulations. Then hire an experienced general contractor to supervise the work.

## Environment Requirements

Besides the raw square footage of your office space, you'll also need to consider what environment you need:

✿ **Should the room be quiet, so you can make telephone calls with some sort of professional decorum?** If so, you will want to be in a separate room so that other household members won't feel like they have to tiptoe around you. You also won't want to be anywhere near your washer and dryer or other noise-generating appliances.

✿ **Will the equipment or inventory stored in the office be very valuable?** If so, stay away from basements that flood and attics that leak. (Most homeowner insurance policies won't cover losses from a business without special policy add-on coverage, but I'll get to that later in the book.)

✿ **Do you anticipate problems with other household members interrupting you during your workday?** If so, choose a room that's at the far end of the home, ideally one with a door that locks.

✿ **Do you want to be near a window?** Some people find a window distracting; they find themselves gazing out the window watching the world go by instead of getting things done. Other people feel like they can't be their best without a little sunlight and connection to the outside world.

✪ **Will you need a place to meet clients?** If so, you'll want a nicely appointed room, with (at the minimum) freshly painted walls, adequate lighting, and clean carpet or flooring. Actually, you will probably want all those things anyway for your own comfort, but when clients get involved, it becomes more critical to have an office space that doesn't embarrass you. You should also consider how clients will get into your office; they shouldn't have to traipse through a bedroom to get there.

**NOTE**   Keep in mind that you don't necessarily have to meet clients in your office. You can use your dining room table or living room, or meet clients at their own offices or at a restaurant. If you live in an apartment or condo, you might also have a clubhouse or public room available. You can also rent conference rooms in real office buildings in many cities.

✪ **Will you be using a lot of equipment requiring electricity?** If so, you'll need a space with lots of electrical outlets. You can use extension cords and power strips to a limited extent, but be careful of overloading a circuit. Homes are not usually designed with robust enough electrical systems to support lots of industrial-strength electrical equipment

---

### THE IMPORTANCE OF ELECTRICITY

When I first set up my office, I had a lot of computer equipment, and I was periodically experiencing brownouts in my office—periods where the lights would dim and some of my equipment would lose power. I had to call an electrician and have him rewire some of the electrical system in my home so that the outlets in the office were on a circuit all by themselves, separate from the rest of the house. Now I don't have to worry about my copier going haywire when someone turns on the microwave in the kitchen.

## Media Jacks

Besides electricity, you will probably also need jacks that connect you to the outside world. The most common of these is telephone, but you might also want a computer network jack (to connect to a computer in another part of the house) or a cable jack (for a cable Internet connection). Think about installing these jacks now, before a lot of heavy furniture is in the way. I'll talk more about phone, Internet, and other connections in the Saturday evening session.

## Proximity to Family Activities

Decide how close you want to be to the comings and goings of the rest of your household. If you need to keep an eye on children as you work (which, by the way, is not an ideal situation), you might want your office area in the middle of the house, perhaps in a corner of the kitchen or dining room. On the other hand, if you're trying to avoid contact with others during your workday, choose a remote spot, away from the common gathering areas such as the kitchen and family room.

## Tax Considerations

If you plan to deduct your home-office expenses from your federal income taxes, you should choose a well-defined area for your office, such as a room with a door that closes. If you're audited, the IRS might disallow your home-office deduction if you're operating out of a corner of an otherwise-residential room, such as having a desk set up in the corner of the family room.

This room should also be used exclusively for your work; it should not fulfill any household need (such as doubling as a guest room). That way, if you are ever audited, you can confidently claim that the room is a real office, and qualified for the deductions you've taken. I'll explain more about claiming a home-office deduction in the Sunday afternoon session, and in Appendix B, "Taxes: A Concise Guide to Schedule C."

# Floor and Window Coverings

Before you start moving furniture into the room, consider what floor and window coverings you would like. They can make a surprising difference!

Carpeting makes the room less drafty and keeps your feet warm if you work in your bare feet (which I do!). But it also accumulates dust, and if you have a lot of equipment in your office, it can be very difficult to vacuum thoroughly. It's also more difficult to roll a chair across a carpeted floor, and heavy chairs and desks tend to leave imprints in carpeting that can be difficult to fluff back out again when you decide to rearrange things. You can buy chair mats to help with chair mobility, but these tend to tear up the carpeting with their little prongs.

Bare floors can be swept or dusted more easily, but they tend to be cold and to make the room feel draftier. Linoleum also scuffs easily, so when you're moving around the furniture, you need to take care to lift it, not scoot it across the floor. Real tile flooring is nice, but expensive, and feels even colder than linoleum. Hardwood floors provide a rich, luxurious feel but need regular preventive maintenance to stay beautiful, and that can be hard to do with lots of furniture and equipment in the way.

As for the windows: I don't recommend curtains in an office unless noise is a problem. (Heavy drapes provide a certain amount of noise insulation.) They get dusty and faded, and most are not machine-washable, so you must have them dry-cleaned periodically. Instead, go with mini-blinds and perhaps a valance across the top of the window for decoration. Mini-blinds can be readily opened and closed, are simple to dust, and can be taken down and soaked in a bathtub full of soapsuds every six months or so for a thorough cleanup.

# Storage Possibilities

One final thing before you start with the furniture. Where are you going to store your stuff?

If you're operating out of a spare bedroom, you probably have a closet available. That's good news, but a closet is typically one big empty space with a clothes rack across the middle. Consider having shelves built into the closet so it will hold more of the kinds of things that you'll need to store, such as office supplies, copy paper, and inventory.

**TIP**  You can build shelves inexpensively in your closet using wood and screws or nails from the local hardware store. Just screw a horizontal strip of wood 2×2-inches to one side wall of the closet, another one just like it on the opposite side, and rest a thick plywood board between them. Voilá, instant shelf! If you're going to store something heavy on the shelf, add a brace at the mid-point.

Besides the closet space, what else will you use for storage? If you plan to buy a storage unit, such as a file cabinet, bookcase, or credenza, decide beforehand where it will go. These bulky items can easily overtake an office's workspace.

# Understanding Ergonomics

It's almost time to pick out the furnishings, but you'll need to do so with an awareness of ergonomics. *Ergonomics* refers to the proper positioning of your tables, chairs, computers, and other equipment in order to prevent body stress and injury. Your body is your most important business asset. If you can't do your job because your body is giving out, that's just as bad as not being able to do your job for lack of customers.

# Carpal Tunnel Syndrome

The biggest threat for the home worker who spends much of the day in front of a computer is Carpal Tunnel Syndrome, also called Repetitive Stress Syndrome. This is a problem with the tendons in your hands and forearms. You get it from typing (or performing other repetitive movements) for many hours at a time, day after day. Early symptoms are tingling and numbness in the fingers; later it can cause pain along with the numbness, especially at night. It usually requires surgery to cure it, although wearing wrist and hand braces while working can considerably slow down the progression.

When I was working in the book-publishing industry several years ago, there was a joke (dark humor, in this case) that you could tell who had the most seniority by looking for the hand and wrist bandages and scars. Nearly every editor who had been there more than a few years was wearing wrist braces or had already had carpal tunnel surgery. I'm telling you this as a warning—if you work in front of a computer all day, and you don't pay attention to ergonomics, you will probably end up needing carpal tunnel surgery, which is expensive and which sidelines your productivity for several weeks while you heal.

So, what can you do to avoid this scourge? Here are some ideas:

- **Rest your hands and fingers regularly.** Shake them out; flex your fingers; take a five-minute break every 30 minutes or so.

- **Use an ergonomically designed keyboard.** As shown in Figure 2.1, Most of these have a split key area, where half the keys slant to the left and the other half to the right. This helps eliminate the need to turn the wrists unnaturally inward in order to type.

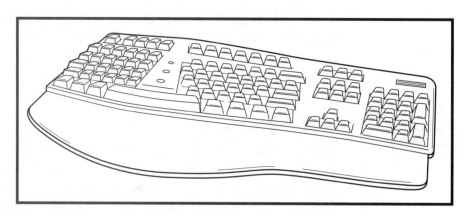

**Figure 2.1**

Ergonomic
keyboard

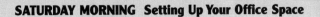

- **Use a trackball instead of a mouse.** My favorite is the Expert Mouse by Kensington, shown in Figure 2.2. (The Mac version is called Turbo Mouse.) It's expensive (around $90), but I love the extra-large ball and the way my thumb falls naturally onto the left button.

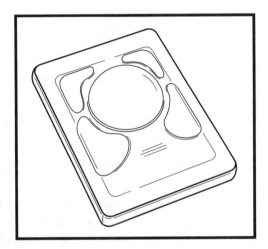

**Figure 2.2**

The Expert Mouse
by Kensington

- **Position your forearms parallel to the ground while typing** (see Figure 2.3). You shouldn't have to reach up to the keyboard. Use a keyboard drawer that pulls out from your desk rather than setting the keyboard directly on the desktop.

- **Try switching the mouse to your other hand.** It might take some time to get used to the action, but it could also stave off Carpal Tunnel surgery for a while if you're having problems with your mouse hand.

## Eye Strain

Those who use a computer a lot might also begin to have eyestrain problems, which can manifest themselves as headaches, blurred vision, bloodshot eyes, and fatigue.

**Figure 2.3**

Arm position diagram

Eyestrain problems are usually the result of poor monitor positioning. The monitor should be placed so that your head tilts down about 5 to 10 degrees in order to view it, and so that it's about 16 to 28 inches away from your face (see Figure 2.4). Start out by sitting at your desk and staring straight ahead. Then stare at the midpoint on your computer screen. Did your eyes move up, or down? If they moved up, lower the monitor, or raise your chair. If they moved down more than just slightly, raise the monitor. (One way is to set it on a book or a small shelf.)

Glare on the monitor screen can also cause eyestrain. One way to prevent it is to place a visor-like hood over the top of the monitor; another is to hang a piece of specially tinted anti-glare glass in front of the screen. But I have found that the best glare preventative is to simply control the lighting in the room. I don't use an overhead light; the single source of light in my office is a large table lamp placed behind and to the side of the monitor. There's no light falling directly on the monitor screen and therefore no glare.

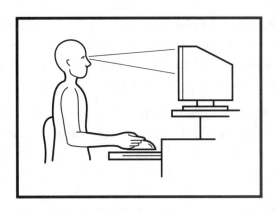

**Figure 2.4**

Correct monitor
positioning

You should also take frequent breaks away from your monitor. Five minutes of every hour should be spent doing something that focuses your eyes at a point that is farther away than your monitor screen. Get up and walk around; look outside; check to see whether the mail has arrived. Do anything, but don't look at your computer screen.

## Back and Neck Problems

Sitting in a chair all day is not in itself a bad thing (although you'll probably want to get some outside exercise!), but many of the office chairs sold today make it difficult to sit with the correct posture needed for a healthy back and neck. Even so-called ergonomic chairs can cause problems if they are not properly adjusted. Most chairs that advertise themselves to be ergonomically designed merely have a lot of different adjustments you can make to them; if you don't make the adjustments correctly, you can actually end up in a worse position than in a non-adjustable chair.

Make sure your chair height is adjusted so that your feet rest flat on the floor, your calves are perpendicular to the floor, and your upper thighs parallel to it (see Figure 2.5). If your chair has lumbar support, adjust it so that it presses comfortably into your lower back.

Neck problems can occur due to poor posture (slouching), but also from trying to cradle the telephone between your ear and your shoulder. If you need to talk on the phone and use your hands at the same time, invest in a headset that you can use with your phone, or use a speakerphone.

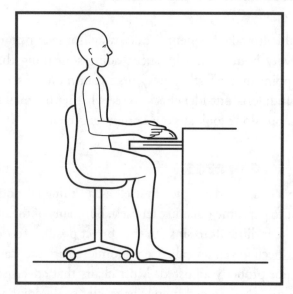

**Figure 2.5**

Proper seating position

# Take a Break

Speaking of taking frequent breaks, how about one now? All that advice in the preceding section can be put to good use. Stretch a little, then come back and I'll give you some advice on how to select the right office furniture.

# Selecting Office Furniture

Start by making a checklist of the furniture you'll need. Use Worksheet 2.1 as a guide. Notice that this table breaks down various work surfaces separately—a desk is separate from a computer workstation, which is separate from a worktable. That's so you can decide how much work surface you need. You might choose to use your desk as both your computer workstation and your worktable, or you might not. It's up to you and your budget.

## Worksheet 2.1  Office Furnishings

| Item | Must Buy | Might Buy | Already Own | Don't Want | Notes |
|---|---|---|---|---|---|
| Desk | | | | | |
| Desk chair | | | | | |
| Computer workstation | | | | | |
| Workstation chair | | | | | |
| Worktable | | | | | |
| Lamps | | | | | |
| Bookcase | | | | | |
| Other storage unit | | | | | |

# Desk

Most home workers spend a great deal of their time sitting at a desk, so it's important to find the best desk for your needs. Many people start out trying to make do with whatever is lying around the house: an old kitchen table, a card table, and so on. But such makeshift desks are seldom suitable for the task at hand. They're typically too high, too wobbly, and do not have any kind of storage drawers.

The top of the desk should be about 30 inches off the ground if you'll spend the majority of the time writing or organizing papers, and 26 inches if you'll use the desk primarily for working on a computer. (See the next section, "Computer Workstation," for help choosing a desk with computing in mind.) The desktop should be large enough to hold the items you plan to keep there, including a computer monitor (if applicable), an inbox, a telephone, and perhaps a stack of organizer trays. But don't go overboard on the size; if your office is small, the desk can overpower the space, limiting the other furniture that can coexist with it. My desk is four feet wide by two and one-half feet deep, and it gives me plenty of room.

When evaluating a desk, pull up a chair to it and sit down. Rest your arms on the desktop. Now reach out as far as you can to the far corners. If you can't touch them, you won't be able to reach whatever you place there; consider whether the desk is larger than you really need.

Next, find a box that's about 20-inches square (if you're in an office supply or furniture store, they probably have cardboard boxes shaped like computers decorating some of the desks in the showroom). Place the box on your desktop. That's how much space a computer monitor will occupy on the desk. Do you still have enough room to write and to spread out some paperwork with that space occupied? (This isn't an issue, of course, if you plan to have a separate computer workstation.)

Many people are attracted to glossy hardwood finishes on the desktop. Such surfaces are very attractive and make a good impression on any clients you work with in your office. However, they're not very durable.

If you leave a cold can of soda pop on the desk, you'll have an unsightly ring. Staples and letter openers can easily scratch a wood finish. Wood is also difficult to clean compared to other finishes; you can't use water on it, and furniture polish can leave it feeling oily.

In my experience, the best desktop is a slightly roughened plastic coating in brown or black. Its nonskid, and you can set drinks directly on it without fear of damage. It also doesn't show dirt or ink marks readily.

Now think about the sides of the desk. Do you want drawers? It's probably a good idea to have at least one drawer in the desk, where you can store small items such as pens and paperclips. Some desks also have a large drawer for hanging folders and a vertical area on one side where you can stand a PC case. If you're planning to use the desk as a computer workstation, and your PC has a tower case (that is, one that stands up vertically), this can be a handy feature; if not, it's merely wasted space.

In addition to your main desk, you might also want a worktable if there is room in your office. A worktable can be used to spread out big projects, such as blueprints, patterns, or craft items. The worktable should be about 30 inches high and sturdy enough that you can't make it wobble without considerable force.

## Computer Workstation

Whether you plan to use a separate computer workstation or you want your computer workstation integrated into your main desk, there are several important considerations.

A brief tour through any office-supply or office-furniture store will reveal a huge array of computer workstation units. These are usually assemble-it-yourself affairs, made out of pressboard wood veneer or some type of hard plastic. It's not that they're bad; it's just that too often they're designed without regard for ergonomics or practical everyday usability.

The first test of a workstation unit is where it allows you to situate the monitor. As I explained back in the ergonomics discussion, the monitor should be positioned so that you look slightly down at it—about 5 to 10 degrees down from parallel to the floor. If you can find a 20-inch cardboard box, set it on the desk to simulate the monitor position. Look directly at the center of it. Where are your eyes? Are they positioned correctly to prevent eyestrain? If not, is there any other spot where you might place the monitor instead that would be better?

**CAUTION**

◆◆◆◆◆◆◆◆◆◆◆◆◆◆◆◆◆◆◆◆◆◆◆◆◆◆◆◆◆◆◆◆◆◆◆◆◆◆◆◆◆

Some computer workstation units provide a special shelf for the monitor, but it's too high for optimal ergonomics. Check whether the monitor shelf is adjustable; if not, see whether you can remove it.

◆◆◆◆◆◆◆◆◆◆◆◆◆◆◆◆◆◆◆◆◆◆◆◆◆◆◆◆◆◆◆◆◆◆◆◆◆◆◆◆◆

Next, check where the keyboard will go. There should be a separate keyboard drawer or platform that pops out from the desk, slightly lower than the desk surface itself. That's because typing with your forearms parallel to the floor takes away some of the stress on your wrists, and such positioning usually requires the keyboard to be lower than the rest of the desk.

And what about the computer case itself? If you have a tower case (a stand-up model), will it sit on the floor at your feet or on the desktop next to the monitor? Make sure there's room wherever you envision it going. Placing the case on the floor saves desk space, but you have to be careful not to kick it over accidentally. If you have a desktop model case (the kind that lies flat on the desk), where will it go? Some computer workstations assume that your monitor will sit on top of a desktop case, but that might put the monitor too high.

Finally, what about other computer-related devices, such as a printer or scanner? Ideally they should be close at hand (especially because the cables that connect them to your computer might not be very long—probably six feet at the most). A good computer workstation should have a shelf on which you can set your printer, and perhaps a second shelf for the scanner or a set of speakers.

**CAUTION** ◆◆◆◆◆◆◆◆◆◆◆◆◆◆◆◆◆◆◆◆◆◆◆◆◆◆◆◆◆◆◆◆◆◆

An important lesson from my own painful experience: Measure the door opening to your office, and don't buy a desk that you can't fit through the doorway.

◆◆◆◆◆◆◆◆◆◆◆◆◆◆◆◆◆◆◆◆◆◆◆◆◆◆◆◆◆◆◆◆◆◆

Use Worksheet 2.2 to record your thoughts on the desk and/or computer workstation you want.

---

**Worksheet 2.2  Desk Features**

| Feature | Notes |
| --- | --- |
| Desired height of desktop | |
| Desired desktop area | |
| Desired desktop finish | |
| Drawers/storage | |
| Area for computer case | |
| Where will your computer monitor sit (if applicable)? | |
| Where will your computer itself sit (if applicable)? | |
| What else will need to set on your desk? | |
| Any requirements for fitting through the office door? | |

# Desk Chair

Your desk chair is probably the most important piece of furniture you'll buy. You'll spend many hours sitting there, so it's essential that it be comfortable and adjustable. As I explained earlier in the chapter, when discussing ergonomics, your sitting position makes a huge difference in your ability to work for long hours at a task without causing undue stress to your body.

All ergonomic chairs are not created equal. A chair that's designed ergonomically to fit an average person is a *static ergonomic* chair and might not have any controls or options for those who don't fit the norm. In contrast, an *active ergonomic* chair provides controls for the back, seat, and arms for customizing the fit for each individual. There's also another kind, the *passive ergonomic* chair, which automatically adjusts to the body of the person who sits in it, either by tilting itself or by raising or lowering itself. These are cool in concept but don't always adjust optimally.

The best way to evaluate a chair is to sit in it, preferably at a desk similar to the one you'll actually be using. Adjust the seat height so that your thighs are perpendicular to the floor and your feet sit flat on the floor. Pay attention to how easy or difficult it is to adjust the seat height, because you might want to adjust the height for different tasks you perform.

 **NOTE** When seated in a chair that's adjusted so your legs are in optimal ergonomic position, measure the distance between the seat and the floor. Then make sure that whatever chair you buy can be adjusted to exactly that height.

While sitting in the chair, notice the edge of the chair seat, where it hits the backs of your legs. Make sure it doesn't have a ridge that digs into your thighs or cuts off their circulation.

Still sitting, lean back. The back of the chair should support the base of your spine, and you should be able to lean back without tipping over. The

chair back should be high enough so that you can rest your shoulder blades on it. A neck or headrest is a bonus but is not really necessary.

Now lean forward as if you were concentrating on a piece of paper on the desk. Try to adjust the chair to tilt forward. Does it have such an adjustment that tilts the seat toward the desk? If so, does it have the capability to lock into that position temporarily? These are good features to have.

Check out the seat that you're sitting on. A soft seat is not necessarily the best because it doesn't help support the base of your spine. A slippery seat isn't good either, because it keeps you continually readjusting your position. A slightly textured fabric makes a good seat, because it's porous and durable. Leather, although it's luxurious-feeling, is not your best value. It is also not very porous, and doesn't let air circulate around you.

The chair arms should be smooth and rather rigid, but not metal. Plastic arms, perhaps lightly padded, work well. The arms should ideally be adjustable, as well, not only up and down but also in and out, to accommodate different body widths.

Now look down at the base of the chair. How many legs does it have? Five is better than four for helping you avoid tipping. If the chair has rollers, look for dual wheel casters (which look like disks), which are better than the ball type (round balls) because they don't cut into flooring and distribute weight more evenly.

Be prepared for sticker shock when you start pricing chairs; a good, fully adjustable desk chair starts at around $400. But don't assume that an expensive chair is necessarily an ergonomically sound one; designer chairs, especially leather ones, are designed to look good rather than to be comfortable for hours on end.

**NOTE**  I stay away from those big black vinyl or leather "executive chairs" that are often on sale at your local office supply store. These look impressive but don't usually offer good back support.

Two years ago, I splurged for an Aeron chair by Herman Miller (see Figure 2.6). It cost me $800 plus shipping. It was the best investment I've ever made in office furniture! This chair is fully adjustable, ergonomically sound in every way, and very durable. Instead of upholstery, it's covered with a breathable mesh fabric that moves along with the body; the arms can be turned inward for keyboarding or outward for writing at a desk. It also comes in three sizes: small, medium, and large. Go to http://www.hmstore.com/ to buy one for yourself. There's a size chart on the Web site that helps you determine which size to get. (If you're between two sizes, go with the larger.)

Worksheet 2.3 will help you evaluate each chair you try out.

**Figure 2.6**

Aeron chair by
Herman Miller

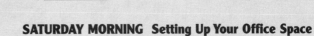

**Worksheet 2.3  Desk Chair Features**

| Feature/Dimension | Yes | No |
|---|---|---|
| Optimal seat height? | | |
| Appropriate chair back height? | | |
| Adjustability? | | |
| Desired seat covering? | | |
| Back support? | | |
| Arm rests? | | |
| Base? | | |
| Rollers/casters? | | |

## File Cabinets

Every office should have at least one file cabinet, with at least two drawers. Even if you don't maintain paperwork on your clients, you can still use the space for keeping paper records of your taxes, the documentation and warranty information for the computer hardware and software you buy, the setup information for your Internet service, and so on. You can get file cabinets with drawers that accommodate either standard paper or legal-size; go with whatever makes the most sense for your business. If you don't have a specific reason to need the legal-size, I recommend standard size because it's cheaper, and the hanging folders you'll likely buy to go inside it will be cheaper too.

You'll find very cheap file cabinets for sale at your local office-supply store, but I encourage you to go with a higher-quality model than the bare minimum. Get one that's constructed of heavy-gauge steel, with drawers that slide smoothly in and out. If confidentiality is an issue, look for a cabinet with a lock on it or the capability to add a lock separately.

Tall file cabinets with four or more drawers use space very efficiently. In a small office, one tall cabinet replacing two shorter ones can free up several square feet of much-needed space. However, keep in mind you'll need to stand up to access the upper drawers (in contrast, you can place a short cabinet next to your desk and use it without getting up).

 **TIP** If you need more workspace but don't want to buy another table, put a board or an old closet door across two short file cabinets.

Some file cabinets have rails on the inside for hanging folders; others don't. You can usually buy rails separately if your cabinet doesn't have one. Not everybody likes hanging folders, however; I have one cabinet with hanging folders and another that simply has a backstop that slides forward to hold my folders in place. I like the latter better.

Most file cabinets have pull out drawers in which the files are stored parallel to the front, but other cabinets store the files perpendicular to the front. These are called *lateral files*. They're popular in large corporate offices because each drawer can hold many more files than a normal cabinet drawer can. However, they're also expensive and big-time space hogs, and they are not suitable for a small home office.

## Other Storage Units

Besides file cabinets, you might also want some extra drawers or boxes in which to store things. I have a stack of plastic drawers on a roller base that I keep next to my desk; it holds paperclips, pens, tape, staplers, scissors, extra floppy disks, and so on. I also have a big wooden storage box under my desk containing extra computer parts that I've accumulated.

If you use a lot of computer software, consider investing in some disk-storage boxes, so you'll always have the disks handy that you need. For example, I have several stacking drawers that hold CD-ROM cases, labeled for various categories of programs (business programs, disks that came with various pieces of hardware, game disks, and so on).

You will probably also want a bookcase in your office for your professional library. That could include any books that you need to do your job, from a dictionary to a reference manual to the Yellow Pages.

Worksheet 2.4 is a checklist of various types of storage units for an office; check off the ones you think you will want for yourself.

## Worksheet 2.4 Storage Checklist

| Unit | Yes | No | Undecided |
|------|-----|-----|-----------|
| 2-drawer file cabinet | | | |
| 3-drawer file cabinet | | | |
| 4- or 5-drawer file cabinet | | | |
| Lateral file cabinet | | | |
| Credenza | | | |
| Bookcase | | | |
| Storage cabinet | | | |
| Stackable shelves | | | |
| Built-in closet shelves | | | |
| Other storage crates or boxes | | | |

# Where to Buy Office Furniture

Your local office-supply store (Staples, Office Depot, Office Max, and the like) is a great place to start looking for office furniture. They typically have dozens of desks, dozens of chairs, and lots of other goodies, such as computer workstations and worktables. Shopping in person is the way to go for most office furniture because you can try it out before you buy and you don't have to pay shipping. (You might have to pay a delivery fee, however, depending on the store and its policies.)

If you're after something specific, such as the Aeron chair I mentioned earlier, you can shop around for the best price. You're not likely to find the best price for a specialty item at your local retailer; check online, searching at one of the major search engines such as http://www. yahoo.com for the item's name and manufacturer. You can also shop for multiple manufacturers and brands at http://www.keysan.com and http://www.officefurniture.net.

# Design and Decor

Generally speaking, I'm opposed to hiring interior designers for home offices. Most people don't meet clients in their home offices, so nobody is going to see the result of all that expense except you. Interior designers also have to be paid, and the items they recommend that you buy are usually fancier and more expensive than the utilitarian but functional items you'll find at your local office furniture outlet.

However, there's nothing wrong with applying some basic design principles yourself as you set up your office:

- ✿ **Wall color.** Choose a neutral, light color for your office walls. A pale beige-tinted white gives the room soft warmth; a blue-tinged white cools it off. But keep it subtle!

- ✿ **Accent colors.** Yellow accents can make you feel more wide-awake and cheerful; blues and greens promote relaxation. Stay away from red and orange; they have a tendency to stress people out.

- **Carpeting.** Wall-to-wall carpeting makes a room look bigger; area rugs do the opposite. Choose a neutral color that'll work even if you decide to redecorate later with different colors. Avoid white or pale carpeting because it shows dirt, and dark carpeting because it shows threads and little pieces of *everything*. Subtle patterns are better than solids unless you plan to vacuum every day. I have a mottled gray carpet in my office, and it never looks dirty no matter how infrequently I get around to vacuuming it.

- **Furniture.** Streamlined, small pieces of furniture can make the room look bigger; heavy, bulky pieces, especially upholstered items, shrink a room.

- **Wall decorations.** You're the one who will be looking at the walls in your office for many hours at a time, so put something on them that you enjoy seeing—a picture of your favorite vacation spot, certificates for awards you've received or certifications you've earned, photos of your family, or anything else that brings a smile to your face.

You might also want to explore feng shui, an oriental interior design practice that helps you choose and arrange items for harmony and energy flow.

Use Worksheet 2.5 to brainstorm your decorating ideas for the office.

### Worksheet 2.5  Design and Decor Ideas

| Item | Decorating to Do |
|------|------------------|
| Floor | |
| Walls | |
| Accents | |
| Window treatments | |
| Decoration | |

# Lighting Your Work Area

How much light do you need? That all depends on what you're doing and on your own preferences. My mother likes a lot of light when she reads, and it drives her crazy to come into a room and see anyone reading with a dim light. People using computers often prefer lower, more indirect light because it doesn't cast a glare on their monitors.

Daylight is often the best lighting, as long as it doesn't create glare. A skylight makes a great "overhead lamp," as does a window. But if you plan to use natural lighting, you must be careful to position your computer monitor so the light isn't coming in directly on it. If your office has a window, put the monitor's back to it, or set the monitor at a right angle to the incoming light.

Daylight is different coming from different directions. Light from the north and south is generally better than from the east and west; it's more consistent throughout the day, and the sun doesn't shine directly into the window in the morning or evening.

If you're remodeling anyway, consider adding a special kind of window to your room called a *clerestory*. These windows are high up on the wall, near the ceiling, and typically run across one or more entire walls. These let sunlight in without letting the sun pour in directly, causing glare. They also offer more privacy than a regular window.

You will probably want to supplement any natural lighting with artificial lights. Overhead lighting can be a good choice as long as it's diffused (again, to avoid glare). A table lamp or a light on a retractable arm has the advantage of spotlighting a particular area when needed without having to be on all the time.

There are two main kinds of light bulbs: incandescent and fluorescent. Incandescent bulbs are the normal light bulbs that go into most lamps and household fixtures. They provide an intense, warm light that's gentle on your eyes and shows colors accurately. The bulbs run hot and burn up

fairly quickly but are cheap to replace. Incandescent light is the preferred kind for homes.

Fluorescent lighting is the preferred kind in most offices because it uses less electricity, runs cool, and uses up bulbs far less quickly than incandescent lighting. It's by nature diffused, so it doesn't cause glare on your computer screen. However, fluorescent lights tend to blink and can cause eyestrain and headaches if you work close to one. They're best for ceiling mountings (the higher the ceilings the better). You can buy fluorescent bulbs that fit into standard incandescent devices, but these can sometimes cause eyestrain too.

If you don't get as much sunshine as you'd like in your office, check out the newer incandescent bulbs that produce light similar to sunlight. These are great for people who get sluggish and depressed in the winter when there's not much sunlight, and they can add a warm, natural feel to your office.

Use Worksheet 2.6 to indicate what lighting you want in your office.

**Worksheet 2.6 Lighting Plans**

| Light Sources | Yes | No | Undecided |
|---|---|---|---|
| Window | | | |
| Skylight/clerestory | | | |
| Incandescent overhead light fixture | | | |
| Fluorescent overhead light fixture | | | |
| Incandescent table lamp | | | |
| Fluorescent table lamp | | | |
| Other | | | |

# Controlling Noise

Which bothers you more, a complete lack of sound or too much sound? Your workspace should balance between the two but lean toward whichever of the extremes is less bothersome to you.

The first kind of sound to control is ambient sound—that is, the sound of your surroundings. This can include the air conditioner or furnace, an air cleaner, a copier, or your computer. Some ideas:

- Turn off equipment that makes noise whenever it's not in use.
- Turn the ringer down on your phone so it doesn't ring so loudly.
- Place noisy equipment in another room, or build a shelf for it in a closet with a door that closes.
- If the weather permits, turn off the air conditioner or furnace while you're working. (You might not want to open windows because that will let noise in from the outside.)
- Carpeting can cut the noise in a room. Choose thick carpeting with a good-quality pad.
- Cover walls with a sound-absorbing material such as cork or fabric. You can buy special fabric-covered panels designed to absorb noise.

Next, there's the incoming noise from outside your office. This can include street noise, children playing, lawns being mowed, your son's stereo from down the hall, and so on. To keep noise out:

- Hang heavy, lined curtains over the windows if your windows are not airtight and soundproof
- Use weather stripping around doors and windows to seal them more tightly.
- Consider replacement windows with double or triple panes. These act as great sound insulators.
- Choose a solid door rather than a hollow one for your office.

**TIP** A few years ago, we replaced our old aluminum-frame windows with vinyl-framed, triple-pane replacement windows. It was the best $5,000 we ever spent. The house is much quieter now, and our heating bill went down by about 20%.

It seems like whenever I get on the phone, my dogs decide to run around the office barking. So far I haven't had a problem with any clients not having a sense of humor about it, but you might have a more urgent need to block out background noise while you're on the telephone. There are devices you can buy for your telephone that will filter out background noise; some phones also have a mute button you can press while you're dealing with some home crisis or irritation during a call.

What if your problem is not enough noise? Don't laugh—this is a real issue. When there is not enough background noise, every little sound seems magnified and pulls your attention away from your work. The neighbor's car pulling out of the driveway suddenly sounds like a dragster. The television set in the family room sounds like it's right there in your office.

You can buy fancy white-noise generators that create background noise—kind of like the sound of an air conditioner running but subtler—that blocks out the sounds that distract you. But you don't have to spend big bucks on that—create your own background noise with an air cleaner (see the next section), some soft music, a fish tank with an air pump, or a computer or printer with a fan that runs all the time.

# Improving Air Quality

The more soundproofing you do, the less fresh the air in your office will be. They're inversely proportional. For clean, fresh air, you'll want to throw the windows wide-open, and leave your office door open at all times.

If your office seems stuffy, try using an air cleaner. These are freestanding units, ranging in size from a breadbox to an ottoman, that plug into an electrical outlet. They suck in the stale air, run it through some filtration, and blow it out again. The primary function of an air cleaner is to remove airborne particles, but many units also have a charcoal filter that removes odors too, so the air smells fresher. Some also have ionization features that charge the air particles to clean the air.

I have a really nice Honeywell HEPA filter air cleaner that does a good job, but I find that it spends most of its time unplugged and stacked in the closet. For one thing, it's rather noisy. For another, it's big, and it takes up about three square feet of floor space that I could otherwise use for walking. So if you're in the market for an air cleaner, consider not only its features and capacity but also where you will put it and whether you will mind the noise. Ask to plug it in at the store, so you can hear how loud it will be.

**NOTE**    An HEPA filter is the most effective kind of air cleaner. They remove 99.97 percent of all airborne particles, down to three microns in size.

Want a less high-tech air cleaner? Buy a plant. Plants, as you know, produce oxygen, so they freshen the air in any room by replacing carbon dioxide with fresh oxygen. Plants can also remove toxins from the air, which build up from household cleaners, cigarette smoke, and natural gas.

If you have problems with nasal or respiratory allergies, especially in the winter, try using a humidifier in your office. Humidifiers pump moisture into the air, and can significantly improve the air quality for those who suffer when the air is too dry.

# Moving On...

Now you're ready to put down this book and go make some purchases! While you're waiting for your new furniture to arrive, go on to the Saturday afternoon session, in which you'll make some choices about the computers and other machines you'll need to run your business. You might have to wait to have everything delivered, so you might not be able to complete the entire book this weekend. That's okay. Just pick it up any time you're ready to continue.

# Selecting Computer Equipment

- ✿ Why Do You Need One?
- ✿ What's Inside a Typical Computer?
- ✿ Choosing Computers and Components
- ✿ Comparing Computer Brands
- ✿ Where to Buy Computer Equipment
- ✿ Setting Up Your Computing System
- ✿ Choosing Business Software

**C**omputer equipment is often the largest expense in setting up a home office, so it pays to give it some serious thought.

## Why Do You Need One?

First, why do you think you need a computer for your business? "Because every business needs one" is not the right answer. Every business doesn't necessarily need one.

Employing a computer is useful whenever you have a job to do that computers can do better than people can. One such task is to calculate numbers; the most common business use for a computer is to store financial records. If you plan to do your own bookkeeping, a computer can run a program such as QuickBooks or PeachTree Accounting that can help you organize your income and expenses without math error.

Another thing computers do well: They keep track of large amounts of data without forgetting any of it, so they're also great for keeping a customer database, such as a mailing list for marketing purposes or a record of who bought what. They can also store inventory records, letting you know when you're getting low on a certain item and reminding you to reorder.

Almost all businesses have financial records, customer records, and inventory records, so almost all businesses can potentially use a computer. However, these records can also be kept on paper at a much lesser expense—that's the way people did business for thousands of years before computers were invented, so it's certainly possible!

If your budget is tight, you can start your business without a computer. If you subscribe to the theory that time is money, however, you will eventually want a computer because having one can save you so much time. Imagine printing a sheet of mailing labels, 30 at a time, instead of writing each customer's address by hand on a flyer! Imagine creating an invoice and having the customer's address appear on it automatically, rather than having to look it up. Having a computer can save you literally hundreds and even thousands of hours of record-keeping labor.

**NOTE**    In Friday evening's session, I suggested that you hire out the functions of the business that you weren't comfortable with. If you have decided to hire out your bookkeeping and inventory, having a computer is much less important.

If you plan to do your own advertising and marketing, a computer can be a great help. With a desktop-publishing program such as Microsoft Publisher, you can make your own flyers, brochures, newsletters, and so on. You can also create business cards with a desktop-publishing program, although most people prefer to have these done professionally to avoid the homemade look.

Even if your business is integrally tied to computers, you don't necessarily need a powerhouse PC. For example, my business is writing about computer hardware and software, but I do most of my work on a three-year-old PC that runs at only 400MHz—less than half the speed of the current top-of-the-line model.

# PC or Mac?

Windows-based PCs are much more popular than Macintosh computers, so much so that the term "PC" has become synonymous with the Windows-based variety.

If you are working in the professional graphics arena, a Macintosh might be the best choice for you because Macs are the standard platform in that industry. You will likely be working with clients who will expect files to be in Macintosh format.

Everyone else should go with a Windows-based PC instead. It's not that Windows is necessarily a better system, but it's a more common system. And because it's more common, your clients are more likely to be using it, so you'll be able to exchange files much more easily if you use it too. PCs are also cheaper than Macs for what you get, and there is more and better software available for Windows PCs.

Macs have a reputation of being very easy to use, and that's true. But Windows is pretty easy too; there's not a huge difference in the learning curve between them.

True story: My father, who is retired, wanted a computer, so he started off with a Macintosh because he had heard it was easier. He loved his Mac and had it for several years, but when the time came for a new one, he decided to go with a Windows PC instead, even though it would mean re-learning. Why? Because he was finding that all the software he wanted to run was either not available for the Mac at all or available only by special order.

He also found that the Mac version of a program was often not as good as the Windows version. Because there is less money to be made in selling Mac software, companies often can't attract the best and brightest programmers to work on it. As a result, the Mac version of a popular program is often a cheap imitation of the Windows version. An exception is

in the professional graphics arena. For these programs, such as Photoshop and Adobe Illustrator, the original versions are the Mac versions, and the Windows versions are the afterthought.

# What's Inside a Typical Computer?

Before you can decide what you need, you need to know a little about the pieces that make up a computer system.

A computer can broadly be divided into two parts: its hardware and its software. *Hardware* refers to the physical parts of a PC, usually made of some combination of metal, plastic, silicon chips, and electronics. The *software* is the collection of programs installed on the computer, including the operating system (such as Microsoft Windows) and the applications (such as the word processor, the financial-management program, and so on). Most PC makers allow you to customize the configuration of the PC you buy, so you can choose the exact hardware and software you need. (Macs are less flexible; when you buy a Mac, you probably won't have a lot of choices.)

You might have looked at the ads in your Sunday paper and wondered why one computer costs $1,000 and a computer that looks almost exactly the same costs $2,500. Well, it's all about the parts inside the case. You pay top-dollar for the latest technology, and substantially less for something one or two steps down from the latest technology.

That doesn't make the cheaper PC bad—not at all. These days, even the cheaper PCs are adequate for most casual users. The primary thing you're buying when you pay more for the latest technology is *time*. You're staving off obsolescence for an extra year or two. The $2,500 computer will have a longer useful life because the technology it uses will be able to run the software that comes out a few years from now, whereas the cheaper PC might not be able to.

In the following sections, I'll tell you about the various parts in a PC that contribute to its cost.

◆◆◆◆◆◆◆◆◆◆◆◆◆◆◆◆◆◆◆◆◆◆◆◆◆◆◆◆◆◆◆◆◆◆◆◆◆◆◆◆

**CAUTION** Some PCs come with free scanners or printers. These aren't really free; their cost is included in the price of the bundle. If you don't need a printer or scanner, it's no bargain. Also, the printers and scanners that come with these deals tend to be low-end, and might not provide the quality you are after.

◆◆◆◆◆◆◆◆◆◆◆◆◆◆◆◆◆◆◆◆◆◆◆◆◆◆◆◆◆◆◆◆◆◆◆◆◆◆◆◆

# Processor

The processor, memory, and motherboard act as a team. The processor and memory plug into the motherboard. You don't usually choose a motherboard when picking out a PC; rather, you choose a processor, and an amount of memory, and the PC maker uses a motherboard that will support your choices.

The *processor* is the brain of your computer. The faster the processor, the faster the computer will be able to work overall, and the more expensive the system will be.

Processor speed is measured in *megahertz*, or MHz. Generally speaking, the greater the MHz of the processor, the faster the computer runs. For example, an 800MHz processor runs much faster than a 400MHz processor.

Intel is the leading brand of processor; it makes the very popular Pentium III, of which Celeron is a subset. A competitor is AMD, who makes the Athlon processor. They're widely considered to be just as good as Intel processors, but usually cost less. One thing to watch, though—many companies put AMD processors only in their lower-end, home-based PCs, which tend to use proprietary parts. (I'll explain more about proprietary parts later, and tell you why they are not good.)

• • • • • • • • • • • • • • • • • • • • • • • • • • • • • • • • • • • • • • •

**NOTE** Athlon processors have a technology called 3DNow! that builds in some special capabilities for 3D modeling into the processor, so if you do 3D modeling on your PC as part of your job, consider Athlon.

• • • • • • • • • • • • • • • • • • • • • • • • • • • • • • • • • • • • • • •

# Memory

The processor works very closely with the memory, a.k.a. Random Access Memory (RAM). RAM, measured in megabytes (MB), is where your computer temporarily stores information that's on its way to or from the processor. Generally speaking, the more RAM a computer has, the faster it runs and the more programs you can have open at the same time. When a computer is turned off, the information in RAM is lost. These days, an average system has 64MB of RAM.

Most systems allow you to add more memory later, so if you start out with a small amount of memory in your new PC and then realize you want more, you can easily have it added at a local computer store (or, if you're feeling intrepid, you can add it yourself). Be careful, though, that you buy a PC that uses standard memory; some manufacturers require proprietary memory for later upgrades, and it's almost always very expensive.

There are two kinds of RAM available today in new systems: SDRAM and RDRAM. I won't bore you with the details about them, but SDRAM is an older technology, and it is cheaper. RDRAM is newer, faster, and more expensive. Both look the same physically; they come on little circuit boards called DIMMs (Dual Inline Memory Modules) that plug into the motherboard.

Memory has a speed. It used to be measured in nanoseconds (ns), with lower numbers being better: 60ns memory was better than 70ns. Nowadays, however, you will more likely see memory advertised as 66MHz, 100MHz, or 133MHz in speed, which means it is capable of working with motherboards that have buses (connections to the processor) of that speed. In that case, higher is better; 133MHz memory is faster.

**NOTE**    You can't use 100MHz memory in a 133MHz system, or vice versa. Whatever computer you buy will come with the right speed of memory, so you don't have to worry about making it match.

# Hard Disk

The hard disk stores the startup files for the PC, the operating system, and any programs that you've installed. Physically, it's a set of metal platters encased in a metal box. Its storage space is measured in gigabytes (GB). A gigabyte is a thousand megabytes (MB).

Generally speaking, bigger is better (and more expensive) when it comes to hard disks. However, hard disk technology has advanced so far that monster-size drives—30GB and up—are now available that few casual users will ever need. In addition, hard-disk technology has not changed at the same meteoric rate that processors have. The size and model of the hard disk you choose will not affect your system's future obsolescence much one way or another. If you ever run out of hard disk space, you can simply have another one installed without getting a whole new PC.

# CD-ROM

Almost all PCs come with a CD-ROM drive. A CD-ROM drive's X number measures its speed. Higher is better—for example, a 50X drive is better than a 32X drive. However, it's not important to have the fastest CD-ROM drive possible—the technology is so good these days in CD-ROM drives that anything over 16X will serve you just fine.

**NOTE** Some CD-ROM drives give two measurements, such as 32X/50X. This is part of a "truth in advertising" movement in CD-ROM makers. Rather than reporting the maximum speed as the drive's overall speed, they tell you the actual range of speeds you'll get, depending on where on a disk it is reading at any given moment. You can compare the larger of the two numbers with a single-numbered drive. A 32X/50X drive is approximately the same as another company's 50X drive.

## Other Drives

For extra money, you can add on other drives. Here's a short list:

- ✿ **CD-RW.** Functions as a regular CD-ROM drive, and also enables you to create CDs using special writeable CD blanks. You could use these to make backups of your important data, such as your customer database or your financial records. These have advertised speeds, such as 8x/4x/32x. The first number is its CD-R speed (writing to blanks you can write only once to); the second number is its CD-RW speed (writing to rewritable blanks). The third number is its read speed when functioning as a normal CD-ROM drive.

- ✿ **DVD.** Functions as a regular CD-ROM drive, and also plays DVD data disks and movies on your PC. You need an MPEG decoder card to go with it. This is a cool feature, but not important for most businesses.

- ✿ **ZIP.** Uses 100MB or 250MB cartridges to store data. Something like a little removable hard disk. Can be used for backup, or to exchange files with other PCs that have ZIP drives when the files are too large to fit on a floppy disk.

- ✿ **SuperDisk.** Replaces your normal floppy drive. Functions as a regular floppy drive, and also accepts 120MB super-floppies. Good for backup and for exchanging large files.

- ✿ **Tape drive.** Backs up your important data onto tape cartridges for archiving. Not as popular anymore now that CD-RW drives can do the same thing.

## Video Card

The video card and the monitor work as a team. Almost all video cards these days have a VGA interface (a 15-pin connector), as do almost all monitors, so any monitor will work with pretty much any video card. Some video cards also have extra outputs for RGB connectors that go to TV sets and other display units, like projectors.

The video card acts as an interface between the computer and the display monitor. Most of the video cards produced today are complete overkill, with more capability and more features than you would ever need. The exception would be if you want a business PC that will also double as a gaming machine, with those shoot-em-up 3D games; then you'll want the best video card you can get. The same goes for graphics professionals. But the average business user doesn't need an expensive video card.

Video cards come with a certain amount of memory on them. The memory doesn't have anything to do with their speed or performance; it's purely a matter of what screen resolutions and color depths they can display. A 4MB video card can display 16.7 million colors at 1024×768 resolution, which should be enough for just about anybody, but most systems these days come with 16 or even 32MB video cards. No biggie—the extra memory doesn't hurt anything.

There are two kinds of slots a video card can plug into on a motherboard.

- ✿ **AGP.** Motherboards have only one AGP slot, and it's specifically for the video card. AGP is a very fast bus (that is, connection to the processor), so AGP video is best.

- ✿ **PCI.** A motherboard typically has several PCI slots, and most of the add-on circuit boards are PCI. PCI video is okay, but not as good as AGP.

◆ ◆ ◆ ◆ ◆ ◆ ◆ ◆ ◆ ◆ ◆ ◆ ◆ ◆ ◆ ◆ ◆ ◆ ◆ ◆ ◆ ◆ ◆ ◆ ◆ ◆ ◆ ◆ ◆ ◆ ◆ ◆ ◆ ◆ ◆ ◆ ◆ ◆ ◆

**CAUTION** Some systems, especially those designed for home users, have an AGP video card built into the motherboard. This saves on the cost of manufacturing the system, which in turn makes the PC cheaper for you, but it takes away some flexibility for future upgrading. You might be able to disable the onboard video card and add another, but such motherboards usually don't come with a real AGP slot, so you'll be stuck using the slower PCI interface for the video card you add.

◆ ◆ ◆ ◆ ◆ ◆ ◆ ◆ ◆ ◆ ◆ ◆ ◆ ◆ ◆ ◆ ◆ ◆ ◆ ◆ ◆ ◆ ◆ ◆ ◆ ◆ ◆ ◆ ◆ ◆ ◆ ◆ ◆ ◆ ◆ ◆ ◆ ◆ ◆

## Peripheral Devices

There are other pieces of hardware that aren't physically located inside the box but are still important to your total computing experience. These are called *peripherals* because they are peripheral (that is, not built-in) parts of the system, usually with a separate casing and power supply. They can be divided into two major groups:

- ✿ **Input devices.** These help you get data into the PC. Input devices include keyboards, mice, bar-code readers, scanners, and cameras.
- ✿ **Output devices.** These help you get data out. Output devices include monitors, speakers, and printers.

Some devices are both input and output devices; they enable a two-way exchange of information between your computer and another. Examples include modems and network cards.

The following sections outline some of the peripheral devices you might choose to include in your computer system.

# Choosing Input Devices

How will you get data into your PC? The most common way is to type using a keyboard. You can also use a mouse (especially useful in a graphical operating system such as Windows or the Macintosh OS), or use one of the other input peripherals described in the following sections.

## Keyboard

All computers come with a keyboard, usually a standard, rather generic model. For a few dollars more, you might be able to substitute the standard keyboard with a fancier one. Special keyboards fall into two categories: those with extra keys and those with unusual shapes that supposedly prevent wrist problems. Some models have both features.

My favorite special keyboard is the Microsoft Natural keyboard. It has some special Windows keys that open menus with the touch of the key,

but the best part is that the keyboard is slightly split so that your hands can lie at a natural angle to type. It also has a built-in wrist rest at the bottom. Generic keyboards with the same features cost slightly less, but if the price difference is small, I prefer to go with the name-brand product.

You can also get keyboards with cordless mice, keyboards with trackballs, and keyboards with touchpads. There are keyboards that are completely split into two pieces, and keyboards that slant up or down. Walk through a computer store's keyboard aisle sometime and marvel at the variety.

# Mouse

A standard mouse comes with almost all PCs. For a little more money, you can have one of the following variations instead:

- **Optical mouse**. It looks like a regular mouse, but it doesn't have a roller ball on the bottom. Instead, it has a light beam that senses movement. Therefore it doesn't get all dirty and gummed up, and it lasts longer. What a great invention! Someone should have thought of this years ago.

- **Cordless mouse**. This is like a regular mouse, but without the "tail" that connects it to the PC. Instead, it communicates with your PC through an infrared beam or radio waves. Most models require you to install a special receiver in your PC.

- **Trackball**. This is something like an upside-down mouse. The base stays stationary, and you roll a ball with your thumb or hand to move the mouse cursor on the screen. My favorite model is the Kensington Expert Mouse, which I showed you a picture of in the Saturday morning section on ergonomics.

- **Touchpad**. These small rectangular pads are built into many laptop computers, but you can also buy them to plug into a desktop computer's mouse port. You just glide your finger across the pad to move the pointer, and tap the pad to click or double-click. I have one of these on my laptop and I like it a lot.

# Bar-Code Reader

If your business involves inventory, you might want to get a bar-code reader to simplify your data entry. Most models come with their own software that integrates with your database software, so you can check in and check out items by their bar codes. You can also make your own inventory tags on stickers to further organize your inventory.

# Scanners

A scanner can help you move toward a paperless office. It reads writing or drawing from a piece of paper and *digitizes* it (that is, creates a digital image of it in the computer). Some businesses scan the invoices and purchase orders they receive and store them on the computer's hard disk instead of a file cabinet (or in addition, as a backup). A scanner is also handy for importing photographs into the computer for use in marketing or advertising materials.

 **TIP**    If you need to take new pictures specifically for use in a computer program, consider buying a digital camera, described later in this session.

Some scanners come with optical character recognition (OCR) software that allows you to scan text and then translate the picture of the text into real text in a word processor. This feature sounds great, but in practice, the OCR software that comes with most scanners makes many mistakes. Some boast 95% accuracy, but what that really means is that, on average, one out of every 20 words will be wrong. You might spend as much time correcting the typos as you would have spent retyping the entire article. If you really need OCR, you can usually upgrade to a professional version of the software, which might be preferable to retyping the original, although still not perfect.

The resolution of a scanner's scanned image is measured in *dots per inch* (dpi), just like printer output. You want a scanner that can scan in at least

300dpi. (This should not be a problem; they all meet that minimum these days.)

You might hear the quality of the scanner expressed as a number of bits, such as 30, 33, or 36. Higher numbers are better, but even a 30-bit scanner will produce good results, so don't pay extra for a fancy scanner unless your business relies on the scanner for its primary product (such as scanning pictures to create Web pages or print materials).

More and more scanners these days have a USB interface. This is a new kind of computer interface that offers many advantages, such as the capability to connect/disconnect devices while the computer is on and the ability to daisy-chain several devices. You must have Windows 98 and a fairly new PC to use it, however, because older PCs don't have USB ports. Other scanner interfaces include parallel (sharing the parallel port with your printer) and SCSI (which requires an interface card you buy separately). If you are buying a new PC with the latest version of Windows, look for a USB scanner.

## Digital Cameras and Video-Capture Devices

If the images you need aren't on a flat piece of paper, then what? Well, you can take a regular photograph and then scan it with your scanner, but you might prefer a more direct solution, such as a digital camera or video-capture device. A realtor might use a digital camera to take pictures of a home, for example, to use on a Web site offering real estate for sale. Or a dog breeder might make video footage of a dog show available on a CD to show potential puppy-buyers.

There is a wide array of devices available to help you put still images and video into your computer. The scanner is one such device, as you just learned; others include digital cameras and video-capture devices.

*Video capture* refers to hooking up a video camera of some sort to your PC and capturing live motion video. You can buy a number of different devices that do this in varying degrees of quality. One such device is a

Connectix, which is a little round ball with a camera lens in the middle and a cord that attaches to your computer. You can point it at whatever you want to record. You can also get interface cards or external adapters, such as a Snappy, that let you attach a normal video camera and feed video into the computer.

A *digital camera*, in contrast, captures still images and feeds them into your PC. Digital cameras are not attached to your PC, so you can take them out into the world with you, just like a regular camera. Then you bring them back to your computer and transfer the pictures you have taken. Some digital cameras hold disks that you can pop out and insert into your PC; others have interface cards that they hook into via a cable, or connect with a serial or USB interface.

Both of these can be a lot of fun, but the models priced so that most small businesses can afford them are not professional-quality, and you might be disappointed with the results. For example, the images taken by a digital camera are fairly low resolution compared to the much sharper images you get when using a regular camera to take a picture and then scanning the results.

# Choosing a Monitor

Monitors come in various sizes. A 17-inch monitor is a fairly standard size these days. 15-inch is an economy model, and 19- or 21-inch falls into the luxury category. Bigger is more expensive, but not always better.

**TIP**   If you are buying a new system to replace an existing one, consider whether you might want to reuse the monitor from your old system. Monitor technology has not advanced very quickly, and your old monitor will probably work just fine as long as it has a 15-pin VGA connector on it that will plug into a modern video card.

When choosing a monitor, keep in mind that it's going to be approximately as deep as it is wide—so a 21-inch monitor will be 21 inches deep.

If you have limited desk space, that might not be the best choice. Some monitors have space-saving designs that make them slightly less deep, but you're still looking at over a foot and a half of your desk depth being occupied.

Most monitors are shadow mask or aperture grille in design. A *shadow mask* monitor is the standard type. I won't go into the details of how it works—just know that such monitors display text and graphics very nicely and are fairly inexpensive. If a monitor doesn't say what kind it is, it's a shadow mask. The other kind, *aperture grille*, is also known as *Trinitron*. It displays richer colors and clearer images, but somewhat less crisp text. Aperture grille monitors also have two faint horizontal stripes running across the display; some people find these distracting.

Monitor quality is measured in *dot pitch* (or *stripe pitch* for aperture grille). A lower number is better, and usually more expensive. A measurement of .27mm is average for dot pitch, or .26mm for aperture grille.

New flat-panel monitors are now available that use a similar technology to that of a laptop screen. These are very expensive (around $1,000 for a 15-inch model), but some people find them worth the expense. They take up almost no depth, so you can place them in a very small workspace.

 The monitor size, measured in inches, is a measure of the diagonal of the glass on the front of the screen. Trouble is, part of that glass is behind the plastic frame (the bezel), and nonviewable. So most monitor manufacturers list two measurements: the monitor size and the viewable area. You might see 17-inch (15.9 viewable), for example.

# Choosing a Printer

Most businesses will need a printer to produce printed output such as invoices, statements, reports, and so on. If you don't have a printer, you can take your work to a local business that rents computers by the hour (Kinkos, for example) and print your work using its printer. You'll find,

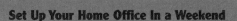

however, that the expense adds up quickly to more than what you would spend on buying your own printer.

## Printer Technology

First, decide what basic printer technology you want: ink-jet or laser. Table 3.1 summarizes the pros and cons of each. An ink-jet printer is initially cheaper, but the ink costs more per page. It's slower than a laser printer, and the output is not quite as good. However, it can print in color, whereas a laser can't (except the very expensive models).

| TABLE 3.1 INK-JET VERSUS LASER | | |
|---|---|---|
| **Considerations** | **Ink-jet** | **Laser** |
| Initial cost | As little as $100 | Typically $400 or more |
| Supplies cost | 5 cents or more per page | About 1 or 2 cents per page |
| Color | Yes | No, unless you buy a very expensive model ($2,000 and up) |
| Print Quality | Good | Better |
| Print Speed | 1 to 8 pages per minute | 4 to 50 pages per minute |

**NOTE**  There is also a third kind of printer technology, dot matrix, which I'll tell you about later in the chapter; it's a an older technology that's useful chiefly for printing multipart forms.

### Ink-jet

Ink-jet printers are the current favorite for most one-person offices because they are inexpensive, produce nearly laser quality output, print fairly quickly (three or more pages per minute usually), and can print in

color. Their only drawback is the high cost of the replacement ink cartridges, which can run $20 or more depending on the model.

If speed is important, look for a printer with a decent pages-per-minute (ppm) rating. For an ink-jet printer, 6ppm for black and white and 3ppm for color is average. The ppm rating is a lot like reported gas mileage for a new car, though—yours might vary and probably will, and not in your favor. It's a good idea to time the printer as it produces something comparable to the work you have in mind in order to decide whether you can live with the speed. Despite the ratings, complex color output can run into minutes per page rather than pages per minute!

You should also consider the ink cartridge system when choosing an ink-jet printer. Ink-jet printers work in one of the following ways, listed from most preferable to least preferable:

- **Four separate cartridges.** One for each color of the three colors that make up all other colors: magenta, cyan, and yellow, and one for black ink. All four cartridges can be loaded into the printer at once.

- **Two cartridges.** One color cartridge that contains each of the three colors in separate compartments, and one black cartridge. Both cartridges can be loaded into the printer at the same time.

- **Two cartridges.** One color cartridge and one black, but only one or the other can be in the printer at a time. When you want to switch between black-and-white and color, you must manually switch the cartridges.

The advantage of having separate ink cartridges for each color, of course, is that you don't waste ink. If you print a lot of red, for instance, the magenta might run out long before the cyan. With a separate cartridge system, you can replace just the colors you use up.

Low-cost ink-jets usually use the two-cartridge method of color printing, whereas more expensive ones give you four cartridges. Printers using the cartridge-switching method are for the most part available only in used-

computer stores. They probably aren't worth the price, no matter how cheap they are. In addition to the extra work of switching the cartridges, they give you very poor copies of photographs. They have to simulate black while printing in color by combining the three colored inks, and the result is a sort of nasty brown.

The cost and availability of the ink cartridges is the final factor to consider. If you buy a well-known printer brand, such as Canon, Epson, or Hewlett-Packard, you will be able to buy cartridges at almost any office-supply store. If you go with an off-brand printer, make sure it can use the same cartridges as a brand-name unit.

## Laser

Before the kinks were worked out of ink-jet technology, laser printers were the only practical choice for business. They are still very popular in business because of their razor-sharp text output and fast, quiet, inexpensive operation.

With a laser printer you are stuck with black-and-white output only, unless you want to spend more than $2,000 on a color model. Upgrading laser-printer technology for color was not a simple matter of revising the ink-delivery system by adding some extra cartridges, as it was for ink-jet printers. The innards of a color laser printer are completely different from those of a regular one.

When shopping for a laser printer, you are interested in several factors:

- **Print quality.** The minimum you should consider is 600dpi (dots per inch).

- **Maximum memory.** Many low-end laser printers come with only 512KB of memory, but you will run into problems printing full-page graphics unless you have at least 1MB of memory in the printer. I wouldn't buy a laser printer with less than 2MB of memory, and even then I'd make sure I could add more memory later.

- **Maximum print speed.** The minimum you should accept is 6ppm; some of the better lasers print 12 or even 20ppm.

You should also check the price of toner cartridges and also check whether your local office supply or computer store keeps the cartridge in stock. For example, I made an expensive mistake when I bought my laser printer a few years ago; I bought a Texas Instruments MicroLaser Pro 600 because it was rated highly in computer magazines. I didn't know it then, but the replacement toner cartridges cost more than $100, and I have to order them by mail because no local stores carry them. Ouch.

## Dot Matrix

There's a third kind of printer available, called *dot matrix*. It works by striking the paper with a series of little pins against a ribbon (like a type-writer ribbon). In many ways, a dot-matrix printer is like an automated typewriter except that instead of letter-shaped hammers, a group of small pins changes position to form each letter.

Dot-matrix printers are impact printers, which means they strike the page physically. Therefore, you can print multipart, carbon-copy forms on a dot-matrix printer. You can't do that on an ink-jet or laser. If you need this capability, a dot-matrix printer is your only option. Otherwise, I would not buy one. You can have a faster, quieter ink-jet printer for just a little bit more money (or maybe even for less money).

## Other Printer Types

You might run across a few other kinds of printers, such as dye sublima-tion, thermal wax transfer, and pen plotter, but these are expensive and not practical choices for most businesses. They are designed for profes-sional-quality color graphic-arts work.

## Multifunction Printers

Several manufacturers have recently introduced a new breed of printer that is designed mainly for small and home offices. The unit combines a print-er and some other device or devices—for example, a fax machine, a copi-er, a scanner, and so on. They go by different names: One manufacturer

calls it a Mopier, another an Officejet. Others simply call them multi-function printers.

These multifunction devices can seem like great values—you get all the functions of several devices for the price (and footprint) of one. The thing to keep in mind is that you're not getting a top-quality example of any of the capabilities. It might print, but probably not as well as a dedicated printer of the same price. It might scan, but not as well as a separate scanner of the same price. You get the idea. They also break down more disastrously than single-function units—the parts aren't unreliable, but when the scanner goes out it's apt to take the printer with it, which wouldn't be the case if they were two separate units. I'm not telling you to avoid these hybrids, but keep in mind that you are trading performance for price and size.

## Printer Speed

The printer's speed depends heavily on the technology that it employs. Dot matrix is the slowest, followed by ink-jet, with lasers at the top of the heap. If you pay enough money, you can have a printer that prints at incredible speeds like 24ppm. Most people have better things to do with their money, though. If you don't plan to print much, a modest 6 to 8ppm is plenty.

Keep in mind that when a printer is advertised at 6ppm, that's its maximum speed—your results will be lower. The 6ppm is the speed that the printer could print, in theory, if it didn't have to process any graphics or wait for the computer to send it any data. In reality, whenever you print a page that contains fonts that are not resident in the printer, or graphics, you will have to wait for the page to come out of the printer. Sometimes you might wait 30 seconds or even a minute for the printer to begin to print. This is normal; don't take your printer back for a refund if it happens.

## Color Printing

Nearly all ink-jet printers sold today are color capable, and nearly all laser printers aren't. So your choice of a color or black-and-white printer is already made when you choose the printer technology you want.

If you plan to print color photographs, get a photographic-quality printer. (Some ink-jets advertise themselves as photographic quality; some don't.) Such printers produce photos well, with vivid colors.

**NOTE** Some ink-jet printers require special paper to produce the highest-quality images. If you pick up a stunning color printout sample at a store, notice whether it is printed on glossy paper. If it is, you won't be able to duplicate that result unless you buy some of that special, expensive paper. Such paper can cost over $1 a sheet!

To evaluate color printing, nothing works better than taking a trip to a big computer store and actually seeing and handling the printouts from various models. You don't have to buy the printer at that store; just look at the samples and then buy the printer wherever it is cheapest.

## Print Quality

Print quality on a dot-matrix printer is not measured very precisely. Printers are either 9-pin (and the output is euphemistically called "near letter quality," which, in fact, it isn't) or 24-pin (for which the output is called "letter quality"). You don't find 9-pin printers for sale new, but you might find a used one tucked away in some used-computer store; don't buy it.

As mentioned previously, quality is measured in dots per inch (dpi) for ink-jets and laser printers. The higher the number, the finer is the quality of the image. Note that in most cases, you worry about dpi only for the sake of the graphics quality; text looks good no matter how many dpi you have.

Most business users will be happy with anything over 600dpi, the most common quality of low-budget laser printers. Most ink-jet printers offer at least 720×720dpi. On ink-jet printers, dpi is given in two separate measurements: vertical and horizontal. You might have an ink-jet printer that prints 1440×720, for example, which means that the printer's vertical resolution is better than its horizontal. (You don't notice the difference; all you notice is that the printout looks a little better than one from a 720×720 printer.)

Some printers offer resolution enhancement, which means they use one trick or another to make the printout seem that it has a higher dpi than it actually does. Once such technology is Hewlett Packard's PhotoRET, which varies the ink-jet dot size to make sharper images. These technologies can make a huge difference in image quality, so don't let the dpi be your only determining factor. Look at sample printouts if possible.

## Fonts and PostScript

Different people will tell you that different things are important about printer fonts, depending on what time period in history they are stuck in. Over the last 10 years, different font-handling schemes have been popular, and various shopping schemes for printers have been appropriate. The sidebar "Whatever Happened to PostScript?" explains the whole gory story.

The bottom line is this: Windows 3.1 and higher, and the Macintosh OS, put dozens of TrueType fonts at your disposal, so you don't need a printer that supports PostScript, comes with lots of built-in fonts, or has cartridge slots. Some wily salesclerk might try to tell you that you need these features, but 99 percent of the time they're a waste of money.

## Printer Memory

Printer memory serves different functions, depending on what kind of printer you have.

## Whatever Happened to PostScript?

Back in the days when all programs were DOS-based, each program had its own font files. For example, I used Ventura Publisher for DOS in 1988, which came with two typefaces: Dutch (similar to today's Times New Roman) and Swiss (similar to today's Arial). When I installed the program, it asked me what sizes I wanted of these typefaces. It then generated font files for each size and variant that I wanted, with separate files for each combination of typeface, size, and attribute (like bold or italic). These font files took up a lot of space on my hard disk. When Ventura Publisher was ready to print, it first sent the appropriate font files over to the printer, and then sent the document to be printed.

Besides using these fonts on disk, you could also use any fonts that were built into your printer. For example, if your printer came with two extra fonts besides Swiss and Dutch, you could also use them in your documents. You could buy cartridges that plugged into your printer and added more fonts to it. I had a 72-font cartridge for my old printer back then, but because each combination of typeface, size, and attribute was considered a separate font, I probably had only three additional typefaces to work with. During this era in printer history, it was important to have a printer with slots that accepted these cartridges. Today, however, printers don't use cartridges at all.

During the same time, if you had $1,000+, you could have had a PostScript printer. A PostScript printer had lots of built-in typefaces, so you didn't need the cartridges. You could also print PostScript-format graphics—a format popular with professional graphic artists—with a PostScript printer. Best of all, the printer used outline-font typefaces, which meant you could use them at any size without having a separate font file on your hard disk for each one. The printer kept an outline of what each letter should look like, expanded or contracted the outline to the desired size, and then filled in the middle to form the letters.

Then along came Windows 3.1, which introduced TrueType fonts. What a revolution! These fonts were outline fonts (like PostScript) that could be resized to any size you wanted. They also worked generically with whatever Windows printer driver you installed, so they worked on any printer, not just a PostScript one. Sales of PostScript printers dropped dramatically because the primary reason people needed them (to have more fonts) went away.

On dot-matrix and ink-jet printers, the printer prints one line at a time on the page as the paper moves through it. Therefore, the printer needs only enough memory to hold one line at a time. That's not much! Any additional memory the printer has serves as a buffer. When the computer tells the printer what to print on the upcoming line before the printer has finished the current line, the extra information waits in the buffer. The larger the buffer, the more data can wait in line. More memory doesn't help the printer function any better for the most part, so the memory amount in an ink-jet or dot-matrix printer is not important.

In contrast, the memory in a laser printer is very important. A laser printer composes the entire page in its memory and then spits it out onto the paper in one pass. Consequently, the printer needs enough memory to hold the entire page. You should have at least 1MB of memory in a laser printer, and more is better. Why? Because memory also has to hold any fonts that the computer sends to the printer. If you are printing a page with lots of different fonts and lots of graphics, you might need more than 1MB of memory for the printer to print it.

## Paper Handling

A good printer should be able to accept at least 100 sheets in its paper tray so you don't have to constantly restock the supply. Nicer models accept up to 250 pages, and some have more than one paper tray.

If you print a lot of correspondence on letterhead, you might want a printer with two paper trays. That way you can put letterhead in one tray and plain paper (or the second page of your letterhead) in the other. Some offices have three or more paper trays on a printer to accommodate the various papers needed. If that sounds appealing to you, look for a printer with good expandability. I have a LexMark Optra S 1855 printer, for example, that can accept a whole stack of paper trays.

# Choosing Multimedia Support

*Multimedia* refers to the system's capability to play music and video. At the minimum, multimedia consists of your CD-ROM drive, a sound card (or built-in sound support), and speakers. It can also include a DVD drive and MPEG decoder card for playing movies on the PC, and add-on devices for recording MIDI music.

A computer for a business does not need multimedia in most cases. Having the ability to play music and video can actually distract you from your work. However, it doesn't hurt to have a no-frills sound card and some small speakers, in case you run across a legitimate business use for sound (such as listening to a tutorial that comes with your new accounting program).

Some systems come with built-in sound on the motherboard; others come with a sound card that plugs into the motherboard. Built-in sound is cheaper, but a separate sound card offers more flexibility for later upgrading.

Today's sound cards provide more than enough capability for the average user, even the very cheap cards. Most business users will be perfectly happy with the cheapest sound card offered by the PC maker. If you can get a system with sound support built into the motherboard, it'll offer the same capability as a basic sound card but might be cheaper than a system with the sound card as a separate unit.

In the past, I have recommended SoundBlaster sound cards, because they were the industry standard that all programs worked with. However, Windows now handles the interface between the sound hardware and your programs, so the brand of sound card is no longer very important.

You will need speakers in order to hear what's coming out of the sound card, but they need not be fancy ones. You'll want them to be amplified speakers, which means they'll need some source of power; this can be either AC or a battery. The cheapest speakers should suffice.

# Choosing a Modem

Do you need Internet access? Probably. Increasingly, the computer world and the online world are merging, to the point where having access to the Internet is one of the primary benefits of PC ownership. With Internet access, you can look up information, post your own Web site, and even start doing business online.

A modem (short for modulator-demodulator) is the traditional way of connecting to the Internet. It uses your telephone line to send and receive information with another computer. However, there are other, faster Internet connections available these days, such as cable and DSL, which you might consider instead. Read the "Internet" section in this evening's session before making up your mind.

If you go with some non-modem Internet connection, you will probably be able to rent the needed equipment from the service provider (your cable or phone company), so you don't need to consider it when buying a PC. For the purpose of the discussion at hand, therefore, I'll assume that you have decided you want a modem.

You can buy the modem with the PC, or separately. If a particular PC comes with a modem already installed, that's great.

All modems sold these days conform to a standard called V.90. It's a protocol for transferring data that can send and receive at speeds up to 56Kbps (that's kilobits per second).

Modems can be internal or external. An internal modem fits into an expansion slot inside the PC; an external modem has its own case and power supply and connects to your PC with a cable. External modems are easier for a rank beginner to set up, but otherwise they're roughly the same. PCs that come with free modems almost always come with the internal variety.

There's a special type of modem designed to work only with Windows, called a *Winmodem*. Avoid them, even if you use Windows exclusively.

Here's why: These modems are cheaper to manufacture than regular modems because they pass off some of the work that the modem normally does to a Windows-based utility program. Keeping that utility running all the time in Windows drains off some of your PC's available memory. You probably won't notice any difference in performance, but it's not a good thing just on principle. In addition, more things can go wrong during setup with a Winmodem than with a normal one—things that a beginner won't know how to troubleshoot, such as resource conflicts. Pay the few dollars more and get a *real* modem. My favorite brand is 3COM/US Robotics.

# Choosing Network Components

If you will have more than one computer in your home office, you might want to network them together so they can easily share files and printers.

The traditional kind of networking is done with Ethernet equipment. To use this type of networking, you'll need a network interface card (NIC) for each computer, a hub, and a cable to run from each NIC to the hub. Look for a Base10T or Base100T network card (go with the 100 if it's not much more expensive; it's faster) for each PC and a five-device hub. You can buy a home-networking kit that contains everything you need to connect two PCs to save yourself the trouble of shopping for the individual components.

AnyPoint Home Networking is the latest thing in networking components. It uses the phone lines in your house to route computer data from one PC to another. This is nice because the computers need not be in the same room, or even on the same floor, and you don't have to stretch cabling out all over your house to connect two distant PCs. Each participating PC requires a special AnyPoint networking card. You can buy a starter kit for this kind of system too, containing everything needed to set up two PCs. Then you can buy additional NICs separately for each additional PC.

# Take a Break

Whew! You've just absorbed a lot of technical information. Take a short break. If you have a techie friend, call him or her and ask for an opinion on the perfect small business computer. Take notes. The answers might not be exactly the same as the recommendations in this book, but they'll probably be close. Then go on to the next section, where I'll give you my suggestions for computer configurations for various business types.

# Your Business Type Determines Your Needs

Obviously, not all home-based businesses will use a computer for the same tasks. Someone who does computer graphical design from home, for example, will want a totally different PC from someone who mostly tunes pianos but wants a computer for record-keeping. In the following sections I'll describe some broad categories of businesses and suggest appropriate computer equipment.

## The Basic Computer System

If you want a computer but don't plan to use it very extensively, you can save some money by economizing on the bells and whistles.

Because the processor is the least upgradeable part, I suggest buying a fairly fast one. Any of the processors sold today will work fine for you, even the cheapest ones, but as I mentioned earlier, buying a faster processor can stave off obsolescence longer.

**NOTE**  I hesitate to say what a fast processor is, because the standards change so quickly that whatever I write will be out of date next week. But as of this writing, processors were available in speeds between 433MHz and 1000MHz (1GHz).

You should also start with a decent amount of memory—say, 64MB. Some cheaper systems come with 32MB, but these days this is not enough, even for the casual user.

You don't need a huge hard disk. An 8GB drive is considered a bit small, but it will do nicely for you. You can always add another hard disk later if you need it.

You don't need a large monitor, because you won't be sitting at it for long hours. A 15-inch model should be fine, but if the system you want comes with a 17-inch monitor, that's okay too.

**TIP** These days most PC manufacturers are trying to convince you that a 17-inch monitor is the minimum size, but that's not true. When customizing your order, ask about switching to a 15-inch monitor if you want to trim $100 to $150 off your order.

As for the other features, such as a CD-RW, a sound card, speakers, and such, skip these unless you have a specific purpose in mind. For example, if you plan to make frequent backups of your data (a good idea), you might add a CD-RW drive to the mix.

You will probably want a modem, for connecting to the Internet. Some systems come with them already, but remember the advice I gave you earlier in the chapter about avoiding Winmodems and sticking with name-brand modems if possible.

You'll need a printer, but keep it cheap. Find a very basic ink-jet printer made by a well-known manufacturer such as Epson, Hewlett-Packard, Lexmark, or Canon.

I went shopping online at Gateway (http://www.gateway.com) and Dell (http://www.dell.com) and found systems similar to the following for about $1,000 that would be a good fit for someone needing a basic, no-frills computer:

- 700MHz Intel Pentium III processor
- 64MB 100MHZ SDRAM
- 17-inch color monitor (15.9-inch viewable area)
- 8MB AGP graphics accelerator
- 15GB Ultra ATA hard drive
- 20X min/48X max CD-ROM drive
- SoundBlaster AudioPCI 128D sound card
- Boston Acoustics digital speakers
- Inexpensive USB ink-jet printer

## The Graphics System

If you will be working with your computer all day creating or editing graphics, you'll need a large, crisp monitor and a video card with lots of memory. You'll also want a big hard disk for storing the images, and lots of RAM.

A high-quality ink-jet printer won't be good enough for printing final output destined for magazines, books, or other professional publications, but you might want an ink-jet printer to print drafts. (Choose ink-jet rather than laser because it can print in color.) If you need a printer that produces professional-quality output, look for a color laser or a thermal wax transfer printer, but be prepared to spend thousands of dollars.

When spending a lot of money for top-notch basic hardware, you will probably not have any money left over for frills such as a sound card and speakers, but that's okay. If there is any money in the budget at all for it, I suggest a rewritable CD-ROM drive (CD-RW), however, because you'll need a way to back up those big graphics files you'll be creating, and CD-RW is one of the best ways. You can also use CD-RW media to transfer files to clients, as huge graphics files won't fit on floppies and can be unwieldy to send as e-mail attachments.

Here's a sample system appropriate for a graphics professional that would cost about $3000:

- AMD Athlon 1000MHz (1GHz) processor with 3DNOW!
- 128MB 100MHz SDRAM
- 21-inch color monitor (20.0-inch viewable area)
- 32MB AGP graphics accelerator
- 20Xmin/48Xmax CD-ROM drive
- 4x/6x/24x CD-RW drive
- Inexpensive color ink-jet printer for printing drafts

If you want a color printer capable of professional-quality output, add a color laser printer to your budget, and figure in another $2000 or more.

## The Portable System

If you need portability, such as the ability to easily take your work on the road with you, a laptop PC is for you. Keep in mind that you'll get much less for your money with a laptop than with a traditional PC and that the latest processor speeds will not be available on laptop models. For example, at the time of this writing, the top processor speed for desktop PCs was 1GHz, but the best laptop you could buy was a 700MHz model. Laptops are also less upgradeable, and more expensive to repair.

 The latest laptops have SpeedStep technology. It allows the computer to slow down its processor speed in order to save battery life whenever the computer is not plugged into an AC outlet. This is a feature of the processor, not the specific brand of computer.

A laptop's price is determined primarily by two factors: its processor speed and its screen size. Laptop screens are very expensive to manufacture, so a laptop with a 15.7-inch screen will be much more expensive than an identical machine with a 12-inch screen.

Some laptops come with built-in modems and/or network adapters. Others require you to buy credit-card-sized PCMCIA devices that plug into a slot on the laptop to provide those capabilities.

A laptop has both an AC power cord and a battery. The best and most modern kind of battery is Lithium Ion. Older or cheaper laptops might have a NiMH battery instead.

When shopping for a laptop PC, let your budget be your guide. Here's a sample low-end laptop for about $1200:

- 12.1-inch HPA SVGA color display
- Intel Celeron processor 466MHz
- 32MB SDRAM
- 8-cell NiMH battery and AC pack
- 6.0GB Ultra ATA hard drive
- Integrated 10Xmin/24Xmax CD-ROM drive
- Built-in internal V.90 56K modem

And here's a high-end one, which costs around $3000:

- 15.7-inch SXGA Active Matrix TFT color display
- Intel Pentium III Processor 700MHz with SpeedStep
- 96MB SDRAM
- 12-cell Lithium Ion battery and AC pack
- 20GB Ultra ATA removable hard drive
- Modular 8X DVD-ROM Drive
- Integrated V.90 56K Modem

# The High-Performance System

If your computer will be the cornerstone of your business, you need a really powerful one, with whatever accessories will be useful to you.

**NOTE** Scared about spending a lot of money on computer equipment? Think of it this way. It's simply a matter of deciding what's really important to the business and then putting the majority of your startup cash into those items. If you will be making money sitting in front of a computer all day, your computer (and your chair) are very important, and you shouldn't skimp on them if you can help it.

For a system at which you'll be working long hours, a 17-inch or 19-inch monitor is a must. The 21-inch models are nice, but remember they take up a lot of space front-to-back, so let your workspace size guide you.

A sound card and speakers are nice, but not essential. I have a basic sound card and cheap speakers, and they serve just fine. It's a business PC, after all, not an entertainment center. DVD isn't important either, but if it comes with the PC, it doesn't hurt anything.

On the other hand, a CD-RW drive is essential. Because your entire business is wrapped up in your PC, you must make frequent backups of important data, and CD-RW is the best way to do it.

The fastest processor isn't necessary, but don't go for the low end either. Your best processor value is probably the one that's one or two steps down from the current top-of-the-line model. At this writing, the top was 1GHz, and the 866MHz processor was a good value, but by the time you read this, those top speeds will have advanced.

Get plenty of RAM. 128MB is about right. Some newer systems come with RDRAM, a faster and more expensive kind of memory. This isn't necessary for you to have right now—the cost is more than the benefit. But watch for it in systems in the next few years, as the price begins to deflate.

Your printer choice depends on how much you'll be printing and what you want the output to look like. Go with a laser printer for high-volume black-and-white; go with an ink-jet for low-volume color.

Here's a sample high-performance business system, which would cost around $2500:

- Intel Pentium III processor 933MHz
- 256MB 133MHz SDRAM
- 45GB 7200RPM Ultra ATA hard drive
- 17-inch color monitor (15.9-inch viewable area)
- 64MB AGP graphics accelerator
- 20Xmin/48Xmax CD-ROM drive
- Recordable/ReWriteable 8x/4x/32x CD-ROM
- SoundBlaster AudioPCI 128D sound card
- Boston Acoustics digital speakers

# Comparing Computer Brands

Now that you know what a computer should contain component-wise, what brand will you choose?

PCs are becoming rather standardized these days. A hard disk, a CD-ROM, a motherboard—these are all components that anyone can buy at a store and cobble together themselves into some sort of functioning computer.

So why don't we all do that? Well, for one thing, we wouldn't be saving any money. Buying individual parts in small quantities can be rather expensive, and many people find that it's cheaper to buy an entire PC, already assembled and configured, than it is to build one themselves. For another thing, when you build a PC yourself, there's no overall warranty. Each part has its own manufacturer's warranty, but when the PC breaks down, you might not be able to determine which part has failed. In contrast, when you buy a PC from a reputable PC maker, technical support is available to help you track down the problem, and their repair service (usually included free in the price of the PC) can fix the problem for you.

# Reliability

When you buy a computer system, the company's name on the front refers to the company that assembled the parts into a system. That company did not make the parts; it bought them from individual part vendors. For example, if you buy a Dell PC, you can bet that the floppy drive was manufactured by one company, the hard disk by another, and so on. However, the PC maker (Dell, in this case) is the responsible party if anything goes wrong with any of those parts. When you buy an already assembled PC, you are also buying the assurance that all the parts will work together without breaking for at least the duration of the warranty.

Because the PC maker doesn't manufacture the parts, it's important that it buys high-quality parts to ensure the overall reliability of the systems. The PC maker wants to make a reliable system as much as you want to buy one, because better reliability means fewer technical-support calls, and less money spent on support staff.

When shopping for a PC maker, you can't call them up and say, "Hey, do you use high-quality parts?" Well, you could, but you wouldn't get a meaningful answer. So instead you need to look at the company's reliability rating in major computer magazines and consumer guides.

Here are some places to start:

| | |
|---|---|
| PC Magazine | http://www.zdnet.com/pcmag/ |
| CNET | http://www.cnet.com/ |
| Consumer Reports | http://www.consumerreports.org/ |

# Flexibility in Ordering

If you buy a PC from a local store, all the configuration decisions have been made for you already. The system has a certain amount of memory, a certain processor, a certain size of hard disk, and so on. But that configuration might not be the perfect one for you.

It's better to buy from a company that lets you customize your PC to the exact specifications you need. For example, you could start with a model that has 64MB of memory, and then up the memory to 128MB by adding a hundred dollars or so to the total cost. That same model might have a writeable CD-ROM drive that you don't need, so you could have it removed and save $150 or so. You get the idea.

The ideal way to customize a computer order is over the Internet, because you can tinker with the configuration, adding a feature here and subtracting one there, to build exactly the PC you want—and you can do it at your leisure, without dealing with a salesperson until you are sure you're ready to buy.

## Standardized Parts

Some computer manufacturers make very sleek, stylized computers that look different from all the other computers on the market today. These are perfectly good computers, but they use proprietary parts—a non-standard floppy drive, an odd-shaped motherboard, or other quirks. If something breaks on them and needs to be replaced when it's out of warranty, you might find it harder to obtain a replacement part if you want to fix it yourself. Even if you take it to a local repair shop, you'll probably pay more for the repair because the shop will have to order the part directly from the original manufacturer and pay full price for it.

If standardized parts are important to you, pay close attention to not only the PC maker you choose, but to the model line you choose from. Some companies, like Gateway 2000, offer a business line of PCs with standardized parts, but also a line of PCs for home use that use proprietary parts.

## Technical-Support Considerations

If you don't understand how to hook something up or are having a problem with the operation, who will you call? Some PC manufacturers have a toll-free number with extended hours and helpful technicians standing

by. Others might require you to make a toll call, and might keep you on hold a long time waiting. Still other manufacturers might not offer phone support at all.

## Warranty

Some bargain PCs come with only a 90- or 180-day warranty, and require you to mail the whole PC back to them for repair (at your own expense!). Look for at least a one-year warranty (two or three is better) and onsite repairs.

If it weren't for the factors explained here, we would all buy the cheapest, generic system we could find. And in fact, that's what some people do— they simply get out the Sunday circulars, find the cheapest PC with the specifications they need, and plunk down the cash. Never mind that it's made with cheaper parts and has a lousy reliability rating. Those people are usually very sorry six months to a year later when they have problems with the PC and pay some technician more money than they originally saved to fix the problems.

## Where to Buy Computer Equipment

Some brands of computers give you only one place to buy them. Dell and Gateway, for example, must be ordered directly from those companies in most cases. (Gateway has begun selling its PCs in a select few retail stores, but that's still the exception.) You can order from the company Web sites or from their toll free phone numbers. Here's the contact information for some of the leading direct PC sellers:

> **Gateway**
> http://www.gateway.com
> 1-800-846-4208
>
> **Dell**
> http://www.dell4me.com
> 1-800-915-3355

**Micron**

http://www.micronpc.com

1-888-224-4247

**Quantex**

http://www.quantex.com

1-800-346-6685

Other brands can be bought in a variety of retail stores such as Best Buy, CompUSA, and others. These include Acer, Hewlett-Packard, and Compaq. These "big three" retail PCs have solid companies behind them but tend toward the stylized cases and proprietary parts that make them expensive and difficult to repair. If the store has an onsite service center with flat rates, that's not a problem, but beware buying a retail-type PC if you don't have an authorized service center nearby.

If you live in an area with a locally owned computer store, you might be able to get a good deal on a "home-brewed" PC constructed right there, especially for you. These local computer stores are usually run buy serious hardware aficionados who prefer good-quality parts, so you don't have to worry about any proprietary junk. And because the store is local, you can take it in for repair or assistance if you have any problems.

# Setting Up Your Computing System

So far in this session, I've taught you about the parts of a computer and what to look for when buying them. But that's all theory. Once you buy a computer, you'll be faced with several large cartons and perhaps no instructions for setting things up. Now what?

First, the good news: Once you get beyond the intimidation factor, PCs are actually very easy to set up. All the plugs fit in only one direction, and fit in only one socket, so it's impossible to make a mistake. Just compare sockets and plugs until you find ones that match. The exceptions are the keyboard and mouse plugs: They both look the same, and can be plugged into each other's sockets (although the PC won't work if you get them

switched). But on most PCs, the sockets are clearly labeled with words or pictures to tell you which is which. If not, check the documentation that came with the PC for assistance.

◆◆◆◆◆◆◆◆◆◆◆◆◆◆◆◆◆◆◆◆◆◆◆◆◆◆◆◆◆◆◆◆◆◆◆◆◆◆◆◆◆◆

Don't connect or disconnect cables to any computer equipment when a device is turned on. Better yet, don't even plug the electrical cords in until you've made all the other connections.

◆◆◆◆◆◆◆◆◆◆◆◆◆◆◆◆◆◆◆◆◆◆◆◆◆◆◆◆◆◆◆◆◆◆◆◆◆◆◆◆◆◆

On almost all new PCs, software comes pre-installed, so you don't need to run any setup programs. Just turn everything on, and you're ready to go.

As I said in Friday evening's session: **you don't have to do everything yourself**. If shopping for a computer or setting it up seems like more than you want to tackle, you can hire someone to do it for you. Computer consultants are available, for anywhere from $50 to $100 an hour, who can select your hardware and software, buy it, bring it to your home office, and set it up.

# Choosing Business Software

Your new PC will probably come with some software. It will have an operating system (such as Windows 98), and probably a few basic utilities, such as an anti-virus program. Depending on where you bought it, and how much you were able to customize its configuration, it might also have some of the other programs you need pre-installed. You will, however, probably need to buy some of your software separately.

In most cases, you can simply insert the new program's CD in your drive and the installation program will start automatically. If that doesn't happen, read the directions that came with the new program for help.

# Office Suite

Most businesses will need word-processing software to compose business letters, write reports, and develop other written documents. Most businesses can also benefit from a spreadsheet program for analyzing numeric data, and a database program for storing information. Such programs can be purchased separately, but are most economical when bought as a group, or *suite*.

Many PCs come with Microsoft Office 2000, the most popular suite in the world. Here are some of the programs you get with Microsoft Office:

- **Word.** A word processing program for writing letters, reports, and other text-based documents
- **Excel.** A spreadsheet program for entering and calculating numbers in rows and columns
- **Outlook.** An e-mail, scheduling, and contact-management program for organizing your business day
- **PowerPoint.** A presentation-creation program for developing slides and handouts for business presentations
- **Access.** A database program for storing and organizing large quantities of data
- **Publisher.** A desktop-publishing program
- **Small Business Tools.** A collection of templates for other programs (such as Excel and Word) that help with business planning
- **FrontPage.** A program for creating Web sites
- **PhotoDraw.** A graphics-creation and graphics-editing program

There are several versions of Microsoft Office 2000; Table 3.2 lists them and tells which programs come with each version.

| Program | Standard | Small Business | Professional | Premium |
|---|---|---|---|---|
| **TABLE 3.2  MICROSOFT OFFICE 2000 VERSIONS** | | | | |
| Word | X | X | X | X |
| Excel | X | X | X | X |
| Outlook | X | X | X | X |
| PowerPoint | X | | X | X |
| Publisher | | X | X | X |
| Sm.Bus.Tools | | X | X | X |
| Access | | | X | X |
| FrontPage | | | | X |
| PhotoDraw | | | | X |

There are other Office suites available that are arguably just as good but much cheaper than Microsoft Office 2000. The two major ones are Corel WordPerfect Suite and Lotus SmartSuite. They have their own versions of each of the tools (word processor, spreadsheet, and so on). Most of these programs save and open in each other's formats, so you can open a Word-Perfect document in Word, for example, and vice versa. However, if you plan to exchange files with one client in particular, it might be easiest to use the same program as him or her.

If you don't need a whole suite, you can buy the programs separately. For example, if you just need a word processor, you can buy Microsoft Word (or Corel WordPerfect or Lotus Word Pro) by itself, as a stand-alone pro-gram, and save yourself some money.

## Accounting Software

Most businesses will also need some accounting software, for those daily financial ins and outs. I like QuickBooks a lot, and find it very easy to use. The other big player is Peachtree Complete. Make sure that the program you choose is powerful enough to handle your financial situation but easy enough that you will be able to learn to use it without a lot of expensive training.

If your accounting needs are very simple, you can get by with an accounting program designed for home use rather than business and save some money. Microsoft Money and Quicken are the two most popular. Quicken has a version called Quicken Home Business that attempts to bridge the gap between the home and home-office user; I haven't used it personally, but it looks like a great idea.

## Business-Planning Software

Lots of companies want to sell you special-purpose business-planning software. Such programs promise to help you write a business plan, develop your customer mailing list, and so on. They're handy in that they often provide tips and ideas that you wouldn't have thought of on your own, but they're also sometimes a bit difficult to use. Personally, I wouldn't spend the money for one of these; I'd use my word processor to write a business plan, my spreadsheet program to add up the numbers, and my database program to keep my customer mailing list.

## Desktop-Publishing Software

If you plan to develop your own advertising/marketing materials, you'll want a desktop-publishing program. Some versions of Microsoft Office come with Microsoft Publisher, which I like a lot. (You can also buy it separately.) Publisher is a nice mix of friendliness and capability and provides templates for everything from spot advertisements to newsletters. Avoid programs that are obviously designed for home use, such as

Microsoft Home Publishing; these won't give you the business results you are seeking.

At the high end of the publishing spectrum is PageMaker. This is a professional desktop-publishing program, with a very high price tag. It doesn't come with many templates or starter ideas, so a beginner-level person will be totally lost. However, an experienced page-layout person will find PageMaker to be a great tool.

## Internet Software

Most people need two kinds of Internet software: a Web browser and an e-mail program. Windows (all versions) comes with both included: Internet Explorer for the Web and Outlook Express for e-mail, so you don't have to buy any Internet software separately.

If you use America Online, the AOL software contains its own e-mail reader and Web browser, so you won't be using the ones in Windows or any other programs.

Internet Explorer is a great, full-featured Web browser. Netscape Navigator is another equally good browser, which you can download for free from http://www.netscape.com. It also has its own integrated e-mail program.

Outlook Express is more than powerful enough for the casual reader and writer of e-mail. If you have Microsoft Office, you also have Outlook, which offers even more e-mail management capability. Most people will never need to move up to the very high-powered e-mail programs such as Eudora Pro; these are primarily for people who send and receive e-mail for a living (mailing list administrators, for example).

# Moving On...

You have some idea of the computer system you need and the software to run on it, so go ahead and place your order now, or go out to the stores and do a little price comparison. When you've finished ordering your computer equipment, go on to the next session, where we'll talk about the hardware, software, and services you'll need to maintain a connection between your office and the outside world.

# Your Connections to the World

- ✿ Telephone
- ✿ Mail
- ✿ Faxes
- ✿ Internet

No office is an island. Whether you are telecommuting or running your own business, you'll need a way (possibly several ways) to communicate with others. Most people think of the telephone as the primary business communication method, but there are many other methods. In this session, I'll review with you several communication media, and provide some suggestions for making the most of them.

## Telephone

For years, the telephone was the only practical immediate-communication medium available to businesses. Telegrams and telegraphs were too expensive and inconvenient; U.S. Mail was too slow; and e-mail and faxing hadn't been invented yet. (Besides, faxing and e-mail both use the telephone too.) Nowadays it remains the staple of many businesses. Every business needs at least one phone line; some need more.

## How Many Lines?

Many at-home workers start out sharing their home telephone line with their business. But this often isn't the best idea, for a number of reasons.

The primary reason people share a single phone line between home and business is the cost of a second line, but these days second lines actually cost very little—I pay only $12 a month for a second residential line. (I'll discuss the difference between a residential and a business line in a moment.) The actual cost of the second phone line might be even less, because the second line is fully deductible as a business expense. Because most freelancers end up paying more than 40% of their income in taxes (scary but true; I'll break that down on Sunday afternoon for you), the actual cost of a $12-a-month second line is only about $86 a year ($144 a year minus 40%.) That's not much to pay for all the extra convenience that a second line provides.

Sharing a phone line with your home can turn off customers, especially if others in the home sometimes answer the phone besides you. Nobody wants to talk to your teenage son (or worse yet, your six-year-old) when they're calling about an important contract. And of course, nobody wants to get a busy signal because your spouse has decided to have a chat with his or her mother during business hours! If you miss even one customer's business per month due to "phone clog," you've lost more money than it would cost for that second line.

With a separate phone line for business, you also avoid that awkward "how to answer the phone" issue. Nothing turns off a customer more quickly than getting a surly "Hello?" when calling your business. Answer the business line with your business greeting (something like "Thank you for calling Freelancer Bonanza, this is Donna, may I help you?") and your home line with your standard home greeting. You can also have an answering machine or voice-mail system on each of the separate lines, each with appropriate messages.

## Do You Need a Business Line?

Your local telephone company offers two kinds of telephone service: business and residential. Residential is much cheaper. It's available only to residences, of course, not to office buildings; because your home office is in a residence, you should have no problem getting it as long as you list it in your own personal name and not the business name.

So why would anyone with a home office pay extra for a business line? There are several reasons. For one thing, you can list the phone in your business's name, rather than your own, and the phone number will appear in the local phone directory in the Business section instead of the residential. It will also appear in the Yellow Pages. That's a big plus if you expect to get customers through the phone book. Another reason is that most phone companies offer a package of business phone services that you can buy on an a-la-carte basis. For example, you might choose to have three phone lines, all on the same number, so that calls can ring through to the second and third lines whenever the first line is busy. Such services are not normally available to residential customers.

## Do You Need a Data Line?

Later in this session, I'll talk about Internet connectivity. If you decide to go with a regular modem connection to the Internet, you won't be able to use your phone line while you're connected. So it makes a lot of sense to get a second phone line (a residential line should be fine for this) specifically for the modem's use. That way none of your voice lines will be tied up while you check your stock prices or send your e-mail.

If you have a fax machine, that's still another reason for a separate phone line. If you don't have a separate phone line for faxing, people who want to fax something to you will have to call you in advance and tell you to switch the phone line over to the fax machine. What a pain! Not to mention how unprofessional it seems.

Some people have a phone line for the fax and the Internet connection to share. This is a good compromise if you don't use either of those services too extensively. People trying to fax you something are usually a lot more patient than people trying to call you by voice. If the line is busy, they will simply call back later. Some fax machines can even be set up to automatically redial and try to resend a fax every few minutes until it goes through.

## Do You Need a Toll-Free Line?

If a large chunk of your business will be coming from customers placing incoming calls to you, consider a toll-free number. Offering to pay for the customer's call in this way builds good will, and might result in more calls than if you had a regular phone number only.

Check with your local phone company's Business Services department to find out the cost of a toll-free number in your area.

♦ ♦ ♦ ♦ ♦ ♦ ♦ ♦ ♦ ♦ ♦ ♦ ♦ ♦ ♦ ♦ ♦ ♦ ♦ ♦ ♦ ♦ ♦ ♦ ♦ ♦ ♦ ♦ ♦ ♦ ♦ ♦ ♦ ♦ ♦ ♦ ♦ ♦ ♦ ♦ ♦

Toll-free numbers can be called only from within the United States. If you plan to have international customers, make sure you publish your regular toll number along with your toll-free number in all your advertisements.

♦ ♦ ♦ ♦ ♦ ♦ ♦ ♦ ♦ ♦ ♦ ♦ ♦ ♦ ♦ ♦ ♦ ♦ ♦ ♦ ♦ ♦ ♦ ♦ ♦ ♦ ♦ ♦ ♦ ♦ ♦ ♦ ♦ ♦ ♦ ♦ ♦ ♦ ♦ ♦

## Do You Need a Cellular Phone or Pager?

If you plan to spend your entire day in your home office, or if your customers seldom phone you with urgent questions or needs, you probably don't need a cell phone or pager. For example, a writer or editor who works at a computer all day would not need one. On the other hand, if you're constantly on the go (for example, in real estate or construction), a cell phone or pager can be a real asset.

So which is better? Well, obviously a cell phone is more flexible and feature-rich. People used to go with pagers because they were less expensive, but cell phones have gotten so inexpensive these days (as little as $10 a month and with a free phone in a recent ad I saw) that there's not much difference. So, all things considered, I would go with the cell phone if available.

I got my first cell phone a few months ago, and before that I felt like I was the only one in the city who didn't already know all about them. I did the research carefully, chose a company, a phone, and a plan that matched my needs, and ended up with a pretty good deal. Here's the process I went through:

## Step 1: Choose a Cellular Service Provider

Each service provider uses only certain phone types, so you need to select your service provider before you buy your phone.

In the metro Indianapolis area where I live, there are several cellular service providers to choose from. In your area, you might have only one. Here are the factors to consider when selecting a provider:

- **Coverage area**. Check out a map showing the areas in which you can receive and make phone calls. Different providers cover different areas. Some are nationwide, but even these have holes or gaps in their coverage. Usually service is centered in metropolitan areas.

- **Analog or digital service**. Analog is an older style of cell-phone service, and tends not to be as clear, especially in non-metro areas. Digital is newer and better. Some service providers offer digital service in their main areas and analog roaming in others (this works only if you have a *dual-band* phone, a phone that supports both analog and digital calling).

- **Roaming agreements**. Even if your service provider doesn't directly support all areas in which you'll be traveling, you might still be able to make and receive calls in outlying areas if your service provider has a roaming agreement with a provider in that area. You might have to pay extra for roaming, but when you need to make an important call, it's worth it.

- **Service plans**. All kinds of rate plans are available, ranging from $10 a month to hundreds per month. Some plans might include extra nights-and-weekends minutes, free long distance, free roaming, free Internet on your phone, or other benefits. My current plan, for example, costs $30 per month and includes 180 anytime minutes, free long distance, and free roaming. Each service provider typically offers several rate plans from which to choose.

- **Special features**. Only one or two service providers in your area might offer some features. For example, perhaps you would like to have two cell phones with two separate numbers but receive only one bill each month and allow the two phones to draw from the same pool of available minutes.

- **Phones available**. If you want a specific style of phone, or you already have a phone you want to use, check out the phones that work with various providers before making your final decision.

- **Commitment**. Some service providers require a one-year or even three-year commitment for a plan. Others let you go month-by-month with no commitment. Generally, the longer the commitment you make, the better the deal you'll get, but avoid signing up for more than one year; the technology will be changing rapidly in the next few years, and any plan that's a good deal now will probably be a terrible deal in three years.

- **Voice mail**. Some service providers offer free voice mail as part of your account; others charge extra for it.

- **Calling features**. Some service providers offer call waiting, caller ID, call forwarding, three-way calling, and other features as part of the monthly fee; others charge extra for them.

## Step 2: Choose a Phone

Next, buy the phone you want. You can usually buy phones at electronics superstores such as Best Buy. You can also buy them at warehouse clubs and kiosks in your local mall. You don't have to sign up for your service plan at the same time that you buy the phone, but most phones work with only one service provider.

Phones can cost as little as 1¢ (with a commitment to a certain rate plan for a year or more) or as much as $300. The cheap phones are usually analog-only models, which are older and not as clear. The expensive phones are typically full-featured with extras such as voice dialing and memo recording, and include wireless Internet browser capabilities.

Here are the features to look for in a phone:

- **Service provider**. Make sure the phone you choose will work with the service provider you've selected.

- **Analog or digital**. Some phones are analog only; others are digital only. The higher-end phones are dual-band, which means they can work in either mode.

- **Address book storage**. Look for a phone that can store your frequently called numbers for easy retrieval.

- **Voice dialing**. Some phones let you dial by speaking the name of the person you want to call. This can be very handy if you call while driving.

- **Data port**. Some phones let you connect a computer modem to them, so you can connect to the Internet on with your laptop computer through your cell phone.

- **Wireless Internet**. Some phones come with a window that displays Internet content, so you can get sports scores, weather, stock quotes, or any other data you need when you're on the road. This feature typically requires signup and an extra monthly fee.

- **Memo recording**. Some phones let you use them as a mini-recorder, recording brief audio reminders to yourself.

- **Distinctive ring.** Some phones let you choose the ringing sound you'll hear, so you can distinguish your phone from the phones of others around you. Some of them can also be set to vibrate instead of ring.

After purchasing a phone, make sure you charge its battery fully before attempting to use it (and before activating it with your service plan, described in the following section). Most phones come with a plug-in battery charger, and you can buy car adapter/charger units and extra batteries through your local retailer or online.

## Step 3: Choose a Service Plan

Finally, you'll choose the plan you want—the price you'll pay per month and the number of minutes and extra features you'll get.

Every provider has its own plans, but see Table 4.1 for some sample ones from a local provider in my area as of June 2000.

Some providers also offer free or extra-charge options with certain plans, such as long-distance, roaming, wireless Internet, additional phones, three-way calling, numeric paging to a phone, voice mail, caller ID, call forwarding, directory assistance, and detailed billing. For example, Sprint PCS (at the time of this writing) lets you choose one of these options for free with your monthly service: long distance, wireless Internet, or extra nights/weekend minutes. If you agree to sign up for a one-year service contract, you get an additional free option such as off-peak, off-network, add-a-phone, or Web messaging.

### TABLE 4.1 SAMPLE CELLULAR PLANS

| Factors | Plan A | Plan B | Plan C | Plan D |
|---|---|---|---|---|
| Cost | $19.99 | $29.99 | $49.99 | $74.99 |
| Minutes | 20 | 180 | 500 | 1,000 |
| Extra minutes | 39¢ | 35¢ | 30¢ | 25¢ |

You'll probably pay a one-time setup fee of about $30, and if you make any changes to your service plan, such as changing to another set of options, you might be subject to a change fee as well.

You can sign up for your service by calling a toll-free number provided by the service provider. You'll need to have your cell phone handy because the operator will need its identification code in order to activate it.

## Standard or Multifunction Phones?

What kind of telephone do you want to use on the primary line you'll use to answer business calls? Some people are content with no-frills phones, the same type they've had for the last 20 years. Such phones are very inexpensive (under $20 in some cases), and work just fine. However, phone technology has greatly advanced in the last several years, and modern phones have features that nobody even dreamed of 20 years ago.

Here are some phone features to shop for, depending on your needs and preferences:

- **Multiple lines.** This is the capability to manage two or more separate phone lines from the same phone.

- **Speakerphone.** This type of phone includes a speaker and microphone that allows you to conduct conversations anywhere in the room without being tied to the handset.

- **Address book.** This feature retains a certain number of phone numbers you program into the phone, for quick dialing.

- **Caller ID.** This is a display that identifies the name and number of incoming calls. Requires caller ID feature activation through your phone company.

- ✿ **Cordless handset.** This feature allows you to carry the handset around the house, rather than being tied to the base unit by a cord.

- ✿ **Volume adjustment.** This allows you to control how loud the caller's voice sounds to you.

- ✿ **Ring adjustment.** This feature enables you to control the volume and/or tone or sound pattern of the ringing.

# Business Telephone Etiquette

I'm always surprised at the number of people who have never been trained in basic business telephone etiquette. The rules for professional conduct on the phone are somewhat different from the rules for polite personal conversations. In the following sections I'll briefly review what you need to know.

## Answering the Phone

When a customer calls your home office, you don't want it to *sound* like a home office. Customers like to deal with people who are doing their jobs full-time, rather than part-time dilettantes, so it's important to sound professional on the phone. You don't want your dogs barking, your children crying, or your dishwasher chugging away in the background. To keep the noise down in my office while I'm on the phone, I shut my office door whenever the phone rings.

When you answer the phone, don't just say "Hello?" Answer the phone with your business name, followed by "May I help you?" Or, if you want to be less formal, or don't have a company name, try "Good morning (or afternoon), this is [your name]."

## Working with Answering Machines and Voice Mail

If possible, don't share an answering machine or voice mail with your family. If you absolutely must share a single phone line, get an answering machine or voice mail system that allows multiple mailboxes for messages. Your opening message can direct callers to, such as this:

> *Hello, you've reached 555-9822. Please press 1 to leave a message for the Smith family, or press 2 to leave a business message for Margo Smith.*

Record a friendly but brief message on your voice mail or answering machine for the business. Here are a few samples:

> *Thank you for calling The PC Helpdesk for the fastest, friendliest computer support and training. We're sorry no one can take your call right now, but please leave your name and number and someone will return your call as soon as possible.*

OR

> *Hello, this is Margo Smith of Smith Accounting services. I'm away from my desk right now, but if you'll leave your name and number, I'll return your call as soon as I get back.*

If you want to make your business sound larger (that is, as if you have more employees than you really do), consider using a commercial answering service. For a small monthly fee, you can forward your calls to the answering service whenever you are away from your desk. The answering service provides a real live operator, who can answer the phone using your company's name, to make it sound like you have a full-time receptionist yourself. Then the operator takes a message and forwards it to you (usually through e-mail or pager).

# Reducing Unwanted Phone Solicitations

Few things are more annoying than telemarketing calls on your business line. Getting a business phone listing rather than a residential one can help in this regard, but a few wily telemarketers might still slip through.

One way to reduce the number of calls you get is to send your name, address, area code, and telephone number to the Direct Marketing Association's Telephone Preference Service (TPS):

> Telephone Preference Service
> Direct Marketing Association
> P.O. Box 9014
> Farmingdale, NY 11735-9014

After a few months, the TPS will reduce the amount of advertising calls you receive from national marketers such as credit card and magazine subscription companies. Some local organizations and charities might not participate. Names remain part of the TPS for five years. After five years, you will need to register with the TPS again.

Also, when you do get a telemarketing call, make sure you tell the person to remove your number from their list and not call you again. They are legally required to keep a list of do-not-call numbers and to abide by that list. There have been instances where consumers have successfully sued telemarketers for $500 to $1,500 for repeated calls after the consumer has asked them to stop calling, under the Consumer Telephone Protection Act.

Some people go so far as to keep meticulous records of each business that calls them, including dates and times, so they can be prepared to take legal action against repeat offenders. This seems a little extreme to me. (You probably have better things to do with your time!) But if you are seriously interested in cataloging telemarketing calls with an eye toward legal action, you might check out Junk Busters (http://www.junk-busters.com), an online organization that helps consumers reduce the

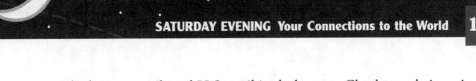

telephone, e-mail, and U.S. mail junk they get. Check out their anti-tele-marketing script at http://www.junkbusters.com/ht/en/script.html. There is also a program called Enigma that offers a script and database for logging telemarketing calls; download it at http://www.antitelemar-keter.com/enigma.htm.

## Mail

The other very common communication medium for businesses is mail delivery. Mail delivered by the U.S. Postal Service is available to all, of course, but there are mail alternatives such as Federal Express and United Parcel Service that have advantages as well.

## Where Will You Receive Your Mail?

Your business needs a mailing address, of course. You can use your home address if you like, or get a separate post office box or mailing address for the business. Here are some pros and cons:

✿ If you use your home address, all your mail comes to the same place, which is very convenient. You can distinguish between business and personal mail by always using the business name as the first line of the address whenever you give out your mailing address.

✿ With a post office box, you're assured a certain amount of privacy; disgruntled customers cannot show up on your doorstep unannounced. However, you must remember to check your box frequently; it's not as convenient as home delivery.

✿ If you want a prestigious mailing address in a fashionable business district of your town, consider a mail service. Your mail is delivered to a service located in an office building, and then the service forwards the mail to you (or you pick it up).

**NOTE** If you use overnight delivery services (discussed more in the next section), you will need to use your street address for receiving packages; most services do not deliver to post office boxes.

# Using Overnight Delivery Services

If your business involves shipping items to customers (for example, if you sell merchandise through a catalog or a Web site), you will need to choose a shipping method. The U.S. Postal Service is certainly a contender, but one of the other shippers might turn out to be a better value because of volume discounts.

 **NOTE** Freelancers working for other companies might also need overnight delivery services, but the company will probably specify a certain shipper and provide an account number to use.

Many shippers offer lower rates to companies that set up an account with them, rather than paying individually for each package at the time of shipment. Having an account number you can charge to is also very handy; you just write the account number on the shipping label of each package you send and then pay one monthly bill for all your shipping that month.

When choosing a shipper, consider the following:

- ✪ **Rates**. Obviously you want to pick a shipper that offers a good value.

- ✪ **Location**. Is there a drop-box near your home for the shipper? It might be worth paying a little extra to avoid driving a long way each time you want to mail something.

- ✪ **Reliability**. Does the shipper have a good reputation for reliable service?

- ✪ **Convenience**. Some shippers offer extras such as Web-based package tracking, free software for printing labels, and so on. These little conveniences can save you a surprising amount of time in the long run.

Here are the major shippers in the United States and their phone numbers and Web sites, so you can compare them and make your decision:

### Federal Express

General Information: http://www.fedex.com

To Open an Account: http://www.fedex.com/us/customer/openaccount/

Customer Service: (800) 463-3339

### United Parcel Service (UPS)

General Information: http://www.ups.com

To Open an Account: (1-800-742-5877)

Customer Service: http://www.ups.com/using/custserv/index.html

Or 1-800-PICK-UPS

### Airborne Express

General Information: http://www.airborne.com

To Open an Account: 1-800-247-2676

Customer Service: 1-800-247-2676

### DHL

General Information: http://www.dhl-usa.com/index

To Open an Account: http://www.dhl-usa.com/account

Or 1-800-CALL-DHL

Customer Service: 1-800-CALL-DHL

# Marketing Your Business through the Mail

I'm not going to turn this into a chapter on marketing—there are lots of excellent small business marketing guides out there. But you can do a lot to promote your business with direct mail.

If your business has a local scope, consider buying ads in local coupon magazines or advertising packets. For example, in my area I get Val-Pak Coupons envelopes every few weeks, with single-sheet ads for a variety of local restaurants and businesses. Buying ad space in one of these mailers can be cost-effective because you don't have to pay for the mailing list, nor do you need to pay for the postage.

You can also market with postcards and individual letters to a targeted group of people, although this can get expensive. Unless you want to market to everyone in your city (in which case you can use the phone book to get names), you'll need to buy a mailing list targeted to your product or service. These typically run about five cents per name. Then you'll either need to print the letters or postcards yourself on your own computer, or hire someone to print them for you. Finally, you'll need to fold, stamp, and seal each one.

If you plan to do a lot of mailing, consider a postage meter, so you don't have to individually stamp each piece. Depending on the volume, a postage meter can also save you a little bit of money because you can mail at bulk postage rates rather than first-class. See your local post office or http://www.usps.com for details.

People get so much junk mail these days (see the following section for dealing with yours) that they often just throw items away unopened, resulting in a very poor return on the investment of sending mass mailings. You can increase your response rate by making your mailing stand out. Here are some ideas:

- Send a brightly colored postcard. Not only is it cheaper, but your message will be read before the card is thrown away. In contrast, when you mail in an envelope, a lot of people won't ever open it to see your message.

- Include a coupon. People tend to save coupons, whereas they throw away all other junk mail.

- If you can afford it, send a cassette tape with a short recorded message or a computer disk with a self-running presentation. People are less likely to throw away tapes and discs than they are paper.

- Send something useful that they'll keep, such as a magnet, a pen, or a Post-It notepad with your company name on it.

## Reducing the Amount of Junk Mail You Receive

If you operate a business from home, you can end up on a lot of junk-mail lists. Once you get on one list, that company invariably sells its list to some other company, and before you know it, your mailbox is clogged with offers. One way to get off the junk mail circuit is to use the Direct Marketing Association's mail preference service. Send your name and address to

Mail Preference Service
Direct Marketing Association
P.O. Box 9008
Farmingdale, NY 11735-9008

After a few months, the MPS will reduce the amount of advertising mail you receive. You will continue to receive mail from companies with which you do business. Names remain part of the MPS for five years. After five years, you will need to register with the MPS again.

If you continue to receive unwanted mail after a few months, you can write directly to each company that sends you mail, asking to be removed from all their lists. You can also call their toll-free numbers if they provide them and request the same.

# Faxes

Faxing revolutionized business communications when it was invented. Suddenly documents could be sent from place to place immediately, without even an overnight delay!

Early fax machines, unfortunately, left a lot to be desired. They used special, expensive thermal paper that came on a roll, and the roll needed to be changed often. Worse yet, if a fax came in while the machine was out of paper, sometimes the machine would accept the fax anyway and you would never see it! Today, however, fax technology has improved greatly. There are plain-paper fax machines available that use the same paper as your printer, and most fax machines have memory built-in that stores incoming faxes until you can reload the paper tray.

 **NOTE** There are two standards for faxing: Class 1 and Class 2. The more recent standard is Class 2. Almost all fax machines today support both standards, however, so this is not a significant shopping point.

# Stand-Alone Fax or Computer Fax/Modem?

Your first decision: Will you buy a stand-alone fax machine, or use a fax-modem in your computer, along with faxing software, to simulate a fax machine? Both have advantages and disadvantages.

A stand-alone fax machine has nothing to do with your computer. It plugs into an electrical outlet and to your telephone line. It automatically answers incoming calls on the phone line (which is why it's nice to have a separate phone line for the fax), receives the faxes, and spits them out on paper. It also has a paper input for faxing pages to others. Some machines require you to feed each page in manually; others have a tray or feed system that lets you insert a stack of pages and walk away.

The advantages of stand-alone faxing? Because it is not tied to your PC, it isn't dependent on your computer being up and running. If a malfunction sidelines your PC, or you forget to turn it on, the fax machine still works. It's also easier to send faxes of hard-copy pages with a stand-alone fax—you just feed them in. (In contrast, with a fax-modem in your PC, you must use a scanner to get the pages into the PC before you can fax them.) And because it isn't connected to your modem, you can use a separate phone line for your fax and your modem.

A fax-modem in your PC does double duty, serving as both a modem (for your Internet connection) and as a fax unit. A single phone line plugs into the fax-modem, so this won't work if you want separate phone lines for faxing and for Internet use. It takes up less space in your office than a regular fax machine, and if it's an internal model, it doesn't require its own power, so you don't have to worry about where to plug it in if outlets are scarce in your office.

A fax-modem makes it very easy to fax documents from your word-processing program, or any other computer program. The fax-modem appears as a printer on the program's list of available output devices; you simply print to the fax-modem to fax the document to the recipient(s) of your choice. In contrast, with a stand-alone fax, you must first print the document, then feed the pages into the fax machine.

## Fax Machine Features

Assume for the moment that you plan to use a stand-alone fax machine (not that that's necessarily the best choice for everyone, but fax-modems have very few distinguishing fax characteristics to shop for, so there's not much to say about them here). Here's a quick look at the features that distinguish one fax machine from another:

- ✿ **Paper type.** Thermal is the older type, and less desirable. Look for a plain-paper fax machine. (But see "Size" below, because thermal is more flexible in terms of page size.)

- ✿ **Size.** This refers to the length of the page you can receive. Thermal faxes can receive documents of any length, because their paper is on a roll and cuts itself at the end of each page. Plain-paper faxes can receive only normal 8.5×11 faxes unless you buy a unit that accepts legal paper.

- ✿ **Resolution**. This refers to the quality of outgoing faxes, measured in dots per inch, or dpi. Most models have a maximum resolution ranging from 200 to 400dpi. You can set up your faxing software to use a lower resolution for everyday use, and switch to the higher resolution (slower faxing) when quality is important for a particular fax.

◆◆◆◆◆◆◆◆◆◆◆◆◆◆◆◆◆◆◆◆◆◆◆◆◆◆◆◆◆◆◆◆◆◆◆◆◆◆◆◆◆

**CAUTION**     Even if you have a high-resolution fax machine, and send your faxes in its highest-quality mode, your recipients will not be able to benefit from it unless their fax machines also support that high resolution.

◆◆◆◆◆◆◆◆◆◆◆◆◆◆◆◆◆◆◆◆◆◆◆◆◆◆◆◆◆◆◆◆◆◆◆◆◆◆◆◆◆

- ✿ **Image enhancement**. Some fax machines have a feature that attempts to improve the quality of incoming faxes.

- ✿ **Paper trays**. To avoid constantly restocking the fax machine's paper tray, look for a unit that accepts at least 200 sheets at a time. Better units will accept up to 500 sheets. Also, if you want the flexibility of being able to accept plain-paper faxes in either legal or letter size, look for a unit with two paper trays.

- ✿ **Incoming fax storage**. Most fax machines will store a limited number of incoming faxes in memory when you are out of paper, and then print them when you reload. The number of pages it can store before it stops answering the phone altogether varies from about eight pages in a budget model to 100 or more in the top models.

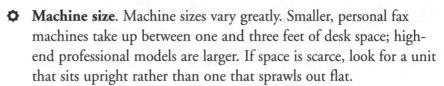

- **Machine size**. Machine sizes vary greatly. Smaller, personal fax machines take up between one and three feet of desk space; high-end professional models are larger. If space is scarce, look for a unit that sits upright rather than one that sprawls out flat.

- **Redial**. Look for a unit that will automatically redial and attempt to send a fax every few minutes until it goes through. That way you don't have to stand around waiting for a recipient's busy signal to go away.

- **Speed dial**. Some fax machines store frequently used numbers for quick dialing. This can save you from having to keep a hard-copy phone list near the fax machine.

- **Broadcasting**. Some fax machines let you send the same fax to multiple recipients without having to feed the pages again. This is easy on a fax-modem, but on a stand-alone unit it requires the machine to hold all the pages in memory, so not all units have this capability.

## Dedicated Fax Line for a Stand-Alone Fax?

If you do a lot of faxing, or if your business depends on customers being able to fax things to you without delay, get a separate phone line for your fax and a stand-alone fax machine.

If you fax only occasionally, you can share your fax line with your data line (that is, your modem). If you use a fax-modem, they're combined anyway. If you use a stand-alone fax machine, simply string phone cable from one device to the next in a daisy-chain fashion. From the wall, run a phone cable to the fax machine. Then from the fax machine's output port, run a phone cable to the modem's input (probably labeled LINE). If you want a telephone on that same line, you can then run a cable from the modem's output to the phone.

## Faxing Software for Fax-Modems

Your faxing experience on your PC depends as much on your faxing software as on your fax-modem itself. When you buy a fax-modem, it probably comes with a simple faxing program, but it might be some off-brand product that's awkward to use. I recommend buying WinFax Pro, an excellent faxing program suitable for business use. WinFax Pro lets you send and receive faxes on your PC either automatically (where the PC answers the phone) or manually (where the PC alerts you of an incoming call and gives you the choice of answering it with the fax-modem or not). It also lets you set up broadcast faxes (in which you send the same fax to multiple recipients) and even run a fax-back service. (More on that shortly.)

## Setting Up a Fax-Back System

Here's a really cool business use for a fax machine: You can store a series of documents, either in your fax machine or on your PC (if you use a fax-modem), and people can dial up your fax line, punch in some numbers to request certain documents, and then receive those documents automatically as faxes. That's called *fax-back*, and many technical-support staffs use such systems to convey frequently requested information to customers. It can also be a terrific way of distributing sales materials.

Fax-back used to be a lot more popular before the advent of the Internet, because the Internet can provide instant access to the same types of documents that fax-back used to uniquely provide. Plus, the Internet can show the data in color, whereas faxing is limited to black-and-white.

If you think you might want to set up fax-back, make sure you buy a stand-alone fax machine or faxing software that supports it. Then prepare all your documents to include and follow the instructions with your equipment or software to set up the system.

# Take a Break

Now that you've gotten your mail, phone, and fax plans mapped out, take a stretch break. The next topic is a big one: Internet business usage. If you don't feel like you have the energy to tackle it right now, put off this next section until tomorrow morning and extend your weekend another day or so. There's no need to rush.

# Internet

Finally, and perhaps most importantly, let's talk about your Internet access. Contrary to popular myth, not all businesses need it. If your business is to provide a service to local residents only, then worldwide advertising on the Internet is not going to be much help. Nor is an e-mail address likely to help a business that doesn't have anything to do with computers, such as a lawn-mower repair shop.

Internet access will cost between $10 and $100 per month (with $20 being the average). You'll need to justify that expense somehow, or it's just a waste of money. Here are some reasons why your business might benefit from Internet access; see if any of them fit your situation.

○ **To communicate with customers and business associates**. Internet access includes e-mail, which can be a cheap and quick way of communicating with others. It's cheaper than long-distance calls, and quicker and cheaper than overnight mail.

○ **To check out your competition**. With Internet access, you can check the Web sites and pricing of your competitors to stay ahead of the game.

○ **To make money**. You can make money from your business online by selling products or services through your Web site. However, setting up a Web site takes time and money, and you might not recoup your investment.

- **To advertise your business**. Even if you don't sell anything online, you can use the Web and e-mail to advertise or market your products and services. However, if your business is locally focused, the Internet is not as good a place to advertise as, for example, a local bulletin board or mailing.

- **To provide a service to your customers**. You can post information about your products or services on a Web site for the free use of your customers. This helps build customer loyalty and appreciation.

There are two levels of Internet access, and you might not need both kinds.

First is the ability to view content on the Web and send and receive e-mail. This is the very basic level, the one that everybody has. You sign up with an Internet service provider (ISP), who assigns you a user name and password and helps you get your software set up. Then you can use a Web browser program to surf the Web (that is, to view Web pages), and an e-mail program to send and receive mail. An account with an ISP typically costs between $10 and $60 a month, depending on the type of service. (More on the service types shortly.)

The second level is the ability to provide content online—to *host* a Web site. Your ISP might offer a certain amount of free server space with your account, but there is probably a restriction on it that prevents you from using it for a business unless you pay extra. Therefore, you'll need to find a site at which to host your Web site (that is, store it on a server so that others can come view it there). Web hosting costs between $10 and hundreds of dollars a month, depending on volume and on the host you choose.

If you want to have a Web site, you'll also need to buy a domain name ($75 for two years, payable up front) and to have your Web site content created. You can do this yourself, but a lot of people find it worthwhile to pay a professional to do the Web development. I'll explain Web development in more detail later in the chapter.

# Choosing an Internet Service Provider

The Internet is everywhere—or at least it seems like it these days. Every time you turn around, someone is trying to sell you Internet access.

There are two basic speed categories of Internet service available:

- A regular dial-up connection with a modem
- Everything else

The former is cheaper, both in terms of the equipment you need for your PC and in the monthly fees, and available nearly everywhere. The other methods are faster, but more expensive and limited in availability area.

**TIP** To find out what kinds of Internet connections are available in your area (cable, DSL, satellite, and so on), go to http://www.getspeed.com and enter your ZIP code.

## Dial-Up Modem Service

For many years, regular dial-up Internet service with a modem was the only connection type available to home users. Large businesses had speedy network connections, but they paid dearly for them—over $1,000 a month in many cases.

Today, there are lots of alternatives, but the humble modem remains the most popular connection type for most home users (and home-office workers too). It's cheap, you don't need expensive equipment for it, and it works in almost all areas.

For a dial-up Internet connection, you need the following equipment:

- A computer
- A modem (V.90 is the current standard)
- A phone jack
- A phone cord

Connect the phone cord from the jack in the wall to the input jack (labeled LINE) on your modem. If you want to share the phone line with a telephone, run a separate phone cord from the output jack on the modem (labeled PHONE) to the phone.

● ● ● ● ● ● ● ● ● ● ● ● ● ● ● ● ● ● ● ● ● ● ● ● ● ● ● ● ● ● ● ● ● ● ● ● ● ● ● ● ●

You don't need a separate phone line for the modem as long as you don't mind not being able to use the phone while you're online. By connecting a phone to the modem's output jack, you allow the phone signal to pass harmlessly through the modem whenever it is not in use.

● ● ● ● ● ● ● ● ● ● ● ● ● ● ● ● ● ● ● ● ● ● ● ● ● ● ● ● ● ● ● ● ● ● ● ● ● ● ● ● ●

Almost all ISPs support regular modems, so you should not have a problem finding an ISP that wants your business.

How do you find an ISP? To find a local one, look in the phone book, or ask around among your friends. If your city has a computer club, contact it or visit its Web site to find out what others recommend. You can also use the Internet Connection wizard in Windows 95/98 to choose from among several national ISPs that Microsoft recommends (in other words, ISPs that have paid a fee to be recommended!).

Only a few years ago, choosing an ISP was a rather arduous task. There were lots of things you needed, like a TCP/IP connection, a POP-compliant mail server, and other techie stuff, and not all ISPs offered them, so you had to ask a series of technical questions when interviewing a potential ISP. Fortunately, those days are over. Any ISP you choose will offer basically the same thing: a TCP/IP connection (that is, a connection you establish using dial-up networking in Windows 95/98/NT/2000) with Web access, newsgroup access, and e-mail access for at least one user name.

But that doesn't mean that all ISPs are equal. It just means that you're now shopping for different criteria. When choosing an ISP, look for the following.

- ✿ **Local access number**. You want an ISP with a local access number for the modem to dial, so you can avoid long-distance charges when connecting. National ISPs provide local access numbers in most cities but not in most small-town and rural areas. If you live outside a metro area, a local ISP might be the only company offering a local access number.

◆ ◆ ◆ ◆ ◆ ◆ ◆ ◆ ◆ ◆ ◆ ◆ ◆ ◆ ◆ ◆ ◆ ◆ ◆ ◆ ◆ ◆ ◆ ◆ ◆ ◆ ◆ ◆ ◆ ◆ ◆ ◆ ◆ ◆ ◆ ◆ ◆ ◆

I'm not saying that a local ISP is necessarily less desirable than a national company—far from it. Your local ISP might be great. But ask around; a bad local ISP can be much worse than a bad national provider in terms of reliability, customer support, and adequate phone lines.

◆ ◆ ◆ ◆ ◆ ◆ ◆ ◆ ◆ ◆ ◆ ◆ ◆ ◆ ◆ ◆ ◆ ◆ ◆ ◆ ◆ ◆ ◆ ◆ ◆ ◆ ◆ ◆ ◆ ◆ ◆ ◆ ◆ ◆ ◆ ◆ ◆ ◆

- ✿ **Customer satisfaction**. Before you choose an ISP, ask everyone you run into what provider they use and whether they are happy. A good ISP is one that you don't notice. With a good ISP, when your modem dials the ISP, it always connects on the first time; you never get hung up on; and when you need technical support, a real person answers the phone promptly. If there's a bad ISP available in your area, chances are good that someone you know is currently struggling with it and would like to unload his or her story on you if you would only ask.

- ✿ **No long-term commitment**. Don't sign up with an ISP that requires a one-year or more commitment. There are many other services that don't shackle you like this, and they're just as good—probably even better. After all, if an ISP offers good service, why would it need to lock in its customers?

✿ **Free commercial Web hosting.** Most ISPs offer to host a small, non-commercial Web site for free for each of their users. However, if you want a Web site for your business, the non-commercial part is a gotcha. You'll probably pay $20 or more extra to host your company's Web site with your ISP (or anywhere else). So if you can find an ISP that will host a small business Web site for no extra charge, you might have found a good deal there.

You can expect to pay about $20 a month for regular dial-up Internet access. I've seen deals as cheap as $10 and as high as $50, all for roughly the same service. Most ISPs give you unlimited connection time for your monthly fee, although some limit you to 120 hours or so and charge you by the minute if you go over that.

◆◆◆◆◆◆◆◆◆◆◆◆◆◆◆◆◆◆◆◆◆◆◆◆◆◆◆◆◆◆◆◆◆◆◆◆◆◆◆◆

When you get a new ISP, you'll have a new e-mail address too. Don't be too quick to have your e-mail address printed on all your stationery and business cards; wait a few months to see if the ISP's service is satisfactory. That way, if you end up needing to change providers, you won't have to reprint all your stationery and cards.

◆◆◆◆◆◆◆◆◆◆◆◆◆◆◆◆◆◆◆◆◆◆◆◆◆◆◆◆◆◆◆◆◆◆◆◆◆◆◆◆

## ISDN

Today's standard for regular modems, V.90, transfers data at about 56Kbps. That's the functional limit for normal phone lines, because they convert the digital data to analog for transmittal, and analog data can't be sent reliably much faster than 65Kbps.

ISDN phone lines get around this limitation. ISDN is a totally different kind of phone line. It's all digital, which means a modem is not needed to convert between digital and analog. Instead, an ISDN terminal adapter (a.k.a. an ISDN modem) sends and receives the digital data. An ISDN line has two data channels and a voice channel, and it can send data at up to 64Kbps per channel, for a total data throughput of up to 128Kbps. That's over twice as fast as a regular modem.

Unfortunately, ISDN has never really caught on. The ISDN phone line doesn't directly support a regular telephone; the phone has to be connected to the ISDN terminal adapter, and the computer has to be on for a phone to operate on the line. The phone line is also rather expensive (about four times the price of a regular phone line in my area), and ISDN terminal adapters can be quirky and difficult to set up in Windows. Besides that, the top speed is only about twice the regular modem speed, and not all ISPs support ISDN. The ones that do typically charge a higher monthly fee for ISDN access.

I don't recommend ISDN service for the average home office user. ISDN would be useful only in a situation where you needed higher-speed Internet access (not just *wanted* it!) and none of the other high-speed options were available.

I had ISDN for two years, and here's what it cost: $60 a month for the ISDN phone line, and $40 a month to my ISP for dual-channel access. (Remember, ISDN has two 64Kbps channels; for fastest speeds you must use both.) I paid over $300 for an ISDN terminal adapter and a high-speed serial port card. That's over $100 a month plus $300 initial setup, and my connection speed wasn't that much better than that of a person who paid $50 for a modem and $20 a month for dial-up service. Conclusion: I paid way too much for way too long. Now I have cable access. (See the "Cable" section later in this chapter for details.)

## DSL

*DSL* stands for *Digital Subscriber Line*. Like ISDN, DSL is a special type of phone service, but unlike ISDN, DSL uses the existing phone wiring in your home or office. You can get DSL service from your local phone company (if they offer it) or from any one of several local and national service providers.

There are several kinds of DSL service, the most common of which are ADSL, SDSL, and HDSL.

The *A* in ADSL stands for asynchronous. With ADSL, the download speed (that is, the speed at which you receive) is faster than the upload speed (that is, the speed at which you send). The *S* in SDSL stands for single-line, and the *H* in HDSL stands for high bit-rate. HDSL and SDSL are both synchronous DSL, so they send and receive at the same rate. The difference: SDSL uses a single twisted pair of wires, whereas HDSL uses two twisted-pair wires, making it much faster (and also more expensive).

DSL works by multiplexing your telephone line into three separate bandwidths, or *frequencies*. Your voice is carried over the lower frequencies (30Hz to 4KHz), leaving the higher frequencies unused. DSL uses those higher frequencies for two-way data transmission. It uses 300KHz to 700KHz to send information, and 1000KHz and above for receiving information. Because it doesn't use the voice portion of the phone line for data, you can use your telephone and be on the Internet at the same time.

DSL speeds range from 144Kbps to over 1Mbps, depending on the class of service you choose. Costs range from around $50 to over $200 per month, and might include free commercial Web site hosting.

When you sign up for DSL service, a technician comes to your house and sets you up, or you get a setup kit in the mail from the service provider with instructions for setting it up. You can buy your terminal adapter if you like, but it's better to pay a monthly fee to rent the terminal adapter from your ISP. For one thing, technology is changing quickly, and today's terminal adapter will probably be worthless in a few years. For another, if something goes wrong with a rented unit, the ISP will replace it, and that's a nice assurance to have.

DSL is pretty cool—and definitely better than ISDN! And the speed is much better than a regular modem connection. But wait—before you decide that DSL is for you, continue reading about the other high-speed access methods: cable and satellite. One of them might be even more appealing.

## Cable

I have to start off this section by saying that I have cable Internet access and I love it. L-O-V-E *love* it. I changed over to cable from ISDN about six months ago, and not only am I saving money, but I'm getting incredible speeds from the thing—over 1.8Mbps on the average, which is better than a corporate T1 line.

For those of you interested in the dollars-and-cents part: Recall that I was spending $100 a month for ISDN. When I changed over to cable, I didn't need the ISDN phone line anymore ($60 a month), so I converted it into a regular analog residential second line ($15 a month). Savings of $45. I decided to keep my old e-mail account with my ISP so I wouldn't have to change e-mail addresses, but I could trim that bill from $40 to $20 because I no longer needed dual-channel access. Savings of $20.

Total savings of $65 a month. Cable access costs $35 a month (with my $5 discount for being a cable TV customer), so I'm saving $30 a month overall, and having a much better Internet experience to boot.

**NOTE**    A T1 line is a big expensive direct Internet connection that companies routinely pay $1,000 or more a month to have. A T3 line is an even bigger, faster version of the same thing. So the fact that I'm getting better speeds than a T1 line on my cable modem at home makes me very happy.

Cable Internet connections are available only for residences, not for office buildings. But because your home office is in a residence, you're eligible if your cable company offers it. Check http://www.getspeed.com to find out whether it's available in your area.

Cable Internet access is cheaper than DSL in my area: $40 a month for cable (or $35 if you are a cable TV customer), as opposed to $50 or more for DSL. It's also faster—in some cases, much faster.

Here's how it works: A cable technician runs a cable to the room in your house where you have the computer set up. (If you already have cable TV from the same company, they split that cable and install a filter to prevent the TV signal from bleeding into your PC's data transfer.) Then the technician installs a network card in your PC and hooks it up to a cable terminal adapter, an external box with its own power supply. The cable from the wall runs to the cable terminal adapter, and then a network cable runs from there to your PC's new network card. Your PC thinks it has direct network access to the Internet—and in a sense, it does. The cable makes you part of the cable TV company's giant network all over the country. Of course, because the cable has nothing to do with your telephone, your Internet access does not interfere with your ability to send and receive phone calls.

Proponents of DSL will try to scare you by saying that cable Internet access slows down as more of your neighbors start using it. And that's true—you probably won't always be able to get 1.8Mbps when everyone on the block is using a cable Internet connection (if indeed that ever happens). But it'll still be pretty darned fast—probably still faster than DSL, as well as cheaper.

Another possible drawback to cable Internet access is that it's always on, and you have a static IP address. (Actually that's the case for DSL too in most cases.) That means that your numeric identifier on the Internet stays the same all the time, rather than being reassigned every time you connect (as with a regular modem). Bottom line: It makes you more vulnerable to hacker attacks. You can easily avoid problems, however, by installing a simple firewall program.

A *firewall* prevents unauthorized access to your PC from outside sources (such as other Internet users). There are various kinds, each working a little differently. There are even hardware-based firewall systems, which are separate little boxes that connect to your PC and monitor all Internet traffic. But you need not get too paranoid, or spend too much, to ensure your online security. I'm running a simple software-based firewall called ZoneAlarm (http://www.zonealarm.com), which is free to individuals, and it works great. Norton Internet Security, which you can buy in computer stores for under $100, includes a firewall program too, as well as some other Internet utilities.

**TIP** You can test the speed of your Internet connection at http://www.computingcentral.com /topics/bandwidth/speedtest500.asp. If you don't routinely get at least 1Mbps from your cable Internet connection, visit http://www.speedguide.net for some tips for adjusting your Windows settings to improve your speed.

## Satellite Internet

Satellite Internet service isn't as good as cable or DSL in terms of speed and low cost, but it works in all areas, even rural ones, so it might be the only high-speed choice for someone who doesn't live in a major metropolitan area.

Hughes Electronics, makers of DirecPC, is currently the only satellite Internet provider. Here's how it works: You sign up for a regular dial-up Internet connection with a local provider, and you also sign up for DirecPC. (DirecPC offers a deal through an already chosen provider for $10 a month if you don't already have a provider.)

You buy a DirecPC satellite dish and put it on your roof (or wherever you can get an unobstructed satellite signal). You hook up the satellite dish to a special network card in your PC. When you connect to the Internet, you upload through your modem, but you download through the satellite. Because the satellite provides nearly instantaneous data, downloading is very fast. Uploading, however, is still limited to your modem's capability (56K).

The speed? Up to 400Kbps. That's better than ISDN and some DSL types, but it is not as good as cable. The cost? Well, your modem ISP will be $10 for the DirecPC-chosen provider or whatever you would normally pay in your area for another provider, and the satellite portion of the service will be around $20. So your total cost is about $30 a month. This low rate has some restrictions, however: You get only 25 hours a month. Additional hours are $2. Go up to 100 hours per month, and the satellite portion costs $35. Go up to 200 hours, and it's $110. So if you use the Internet a lot, satellite access can be very expensive.

Satellite access is not a good choice for city dwellers, generally speaking, because better options are available and because the satellite dish requires an unobstructed line of sight to the southern sky. For someone on a farm in the middle of nowhere, however, it can be the best option available. For more information, see http://www.direcPC.com.

# All About America Online

You have undoubtedly heard of America Online, and you've probably gotten a free sign-up disk or two in the mail.

America Online is an online service rather than an ISP. AOL provides its own copyrighted content, with chat rooms, message boards, news stories, and other features not available elsewhere on the Internet. AOL also has its own e-mail system, and its own Web browser for accessing the Internet. Figure 4.1 shows a sample America Online window.

America Online is great for beginning home users, but not the right choice for a business user. For one thing, it lacks flexibility. You must use the AOL software rather than an e-mail program and Web browser of your own choosing, and e-mail attachments don't always come through correctly when sent or received from outside AOL. That makes it hard to exchange files with customers who are not AOL users.

**Figure 4.1**

America Online, a great service for home use

Another issue is AOL's built-in Web browser. It is based on Internet Explorer, but its controls are not as good, and I have encountered Web pages that opened fine on my PC with a regular ISP that would cause the AOL software to lock up.

AOL remains, at its heart, a community unto itself. It tries to be an ISP by offering some of the same services that an ISP offers, such as Web browsing, but it feels awkward and kludged together. I'm not saying you shouldn't be an AOL member—I'm a member myself—but you shouldn't rely on AOL as your sole method of Internet access for your business.

# Managing Your Time Online

Once you get online, then what? It's important to avoid the tempting distractions online and remember why you decided to get Internet access in the first place: to further your business interests. Toward that end, here are some tips.

## Using Search Engines

Don't spend a lot of time wandering around from site to site on the Web; instead, use one of the many free search engines to locate what you need.

If you use Internet Explorer, your start page (probably http://www. msn.com) offers a Search the Web box, as shown in Figure 4.2; this is an example of a search engine. Simply type a few words into the box and click Search, and a list of sites matching those keywords appears, as shown in Figure 4.3.

Other search engines include the following:

- ✿ http://www.yahoo.com
- ✿ http://www.webcrawler.com
- ✿ http://www.askjeeves.com

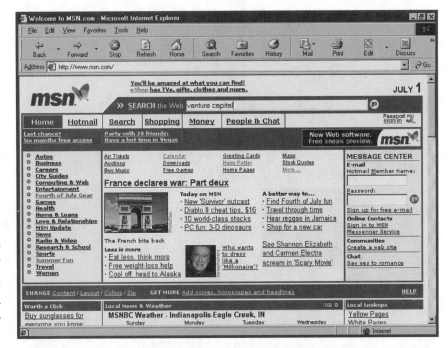

**Figure 4.2**

You can enter keywords to search for at http://www.msn.com or any of several other search sites.

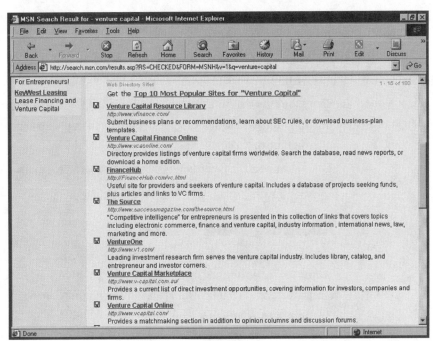

**Figure 4.3**

The results of your search appear in a new page.

- http://www.altavista.com
- http://www.go.com
- http://www.lycos.com

## Sending Business E-mail

You might already be familiar with the mechanics of sending and receiving e-mail, but there are a few extra etiquette rules to obey when using e-mail for business purposes.

To maintain good will when e-mailing customers, vendors, and other people with whom you do business, observe the following rules:

- Use correct capitalization. Don't type in ALL CAPS, and don't type in all lowercase.
- Keep the message brief and to the point.
- Observe simple courtesies such as beginning the message with "Dear [name]" or "Hi [name]!"
- Sign (type) your name at the bottom of the message.
- Don't convey bad or controversial news through e-mail; such information is better delivered through a phone call or an in-person visit.
- Don't try to be funny or ironic in an e-mail; subtle humor often falls flat without person-to-person interpretation of gestures and facial expressions.
- Don't send forwards (such as chain letters, poems, prayers, or cute little cartoons) to business associates.

## Avoiding Junk E-mail

When you check your e-mail, you don't want to be slowed down by a bunch of unsolicited junk. One way to avoid it is to have a separate e-mail address that you use whenever you're prompted to enter your e-mail address on a form you fill out. You can then reserve your main e-mail address for use by your friends and colleagues.

Another way to reduce the amount of junk e-mail you receive is to use the Direct Marketing Association's E-mail Preference Service to remove yourself from several e-mail lists used by mass e-mailers. Go to http://www.e-mps.org/en/ to do so.

# Setting Up a Web Site

So far in this section of the chapter, you've been learning about what it takes to become an Internet user. Now turn your attention to the other side of the equation: becoming an Internet content provider. Your business can have its own Web site that people all over the world can visit. In theory, anyway, millions of people will have access to whatever information you want to provide! In practice, it doesn't work quite that way, because not all of the millions of Internet users (or even one percent of them) will visit your Web site. Still, with the right marketing behind it, a Web site can be an effective tool in publicizing your business and getting new customers.

## Finding a Web Host

You will need space on a Web server to store your Web site. You can't serve up the Web site from your own personal computer because

- You are not connected to the Internet 24/7.
- The traffic might bog down your system to the point where you couldn't use it for anything else.
- Most ISPs won't allow you to do so anyway.

A Web server is simply a computer that's connected full-time to the Internet, and whose only purpose is to store and provide access to Web pages. Your ISP has one, as do specialized companies who do *Web hosting*.

As I mentioned earlier, your ISP probably provides a small amount of free server space to each user, but most ISPs have a restriction on how you can use that space, and business use is usually prohibited unless you pay extra. So you must choose: Will you pay extra to let your ISP host your Web site, or will you go with a Web-hosting company?

**NOTE** Even if your ISP does let you host your business's Web site on its server for free, they probably will not let you use your own domain name for it (discussed in the next section).

When shopping for a Web host, price is a consideration, of course, but not the only one. An average price for Web hosting is $20 to $40 a month for a small Web site (which is what you'll have—initially anyway). Here are some other comparison points:

- **E-mail addresses.** How many separate e-mail addresses do you get? This usually ranges from 10 to 25 or so.

- **Server space.** How much storage space do you get? 50MB is an average amount.

- **UNIX or NT support.** There are two kinds of servers: UNIX and Windows NT. The latter can support FrontPage extensions, so if you create your Web site in FrontPage, you'll want an NT server. Some UNIX servers can support FrontPage too, though, so check around. UNIX servers are usually cheaper per month.

- **Support for specific programs.** If you use programs such as Front-Page, DreamWeaver, or Visual InterDev to create your Web content, make sure the server you choose supports their unique features.

- **Setup fee.** Some Web hosts charge you a one-time fee to get started; others don't.

- **Prepayment discount.** Some Web hosts give you a price break if you pay for six or 12 months in advance.

- **E-mail features.** Some Web hosts provide services such as e-mail forwarding, auto-response, Web-based e-mail, and mailing-list management.

- **Traffic limits.** Some Web hosts have a limit on the amount of traffic (that is, visitors to your site). They charge you extra if there is more than a certain amount of traffic per month (for example, 4000MB per month of data transfer). This is usually not an issue unless your site becomes phenomenally popular.

- **Anonymous FTP.** Some Web hosts let you set up an FTP site that people can visit to download files you have made available (such as demos of a software product you are selling, for example). On UNIX servers, anonymous FTP and FrontPage server extensions (if available) might be mutually exclusive—that is, you might be able to have one or the other but not both.

- **Statistics.** Some Web hosts keep track of the number of visitors to your Web site, and allow you to access detailed reports.

- **Management controls.** Some Web hosts offer Web-based control panels that help you manage your Web site and your domain; others merely provide FTP access to a server to which you upload your Web pages.

## Getting Your Own Domain Name

When you use the free server space provided from your ISP, you're stuck with the ISP's name in your Web site address. For example, If my ISP's name was MyISP, my personal Web site address might be something like this:

http://members.myisp.com/~fwempen

That certainly doesn't look very professional; it looks like I'm a small-time hobbyist who isn't really serious about my business's Web presence.

For only $75, you can get your own domain name—that is, www.*Your-CompanyName*.com. That $75 pays for the first two years, and then after that you can pay year-by-year. When you host your Web site with a Web-hosting company, it expects you to have your own domain name. Some will even register the domain name for you, taking care of all the paper-work to get it processed.

You can get a .com ("commercial"), .org ("organization"), or .net ("Internet") suffix. Most of the good .com names are taken, but you might be able to get the same name in .org or .net. For example, as of this writing, www.FreelanceEditor.com was taken, but FreelanceEditor.org and .net were available.

**NOTE** Web addresses are not case sensitive. FreelanceEditor and freelanceeditor are the same thing. But you can write them with certain letters capitalized (in your marketing materials, for example) to divide a string into words that are easier for your customers to remember.

Lots of Web sites offer a look-up service that tells you what's already taken and what's available. Try http://domreg.ahnet.net , for example.

You register a domain name through InterNIC (http://www.internic.net), but the Web host you choose will probably take care of the registration process for you, so you don't have to go through InterNIC directly.

## Creating Your Web Site

If you are not terribly handy with a computer, and you want a professional-quality Web site, do yourself a favor and hire someone to create it. This is especially true if you plan an ambitious site with online product ordering. The bar for Web sites is rather high these days, because of all the people out there doing professional Web development with expensive software. A Web site you create yourself will probably not hold up favorably against the sites of your competitors. Compare, for example, the Web site in Figure 4.4, which was created by a professional, with the one in Figure 4.5, which is obviously a home-made affair. At which site would *you* feel more comfortable shopping?

On the other hand, if you don't plan to actually do business online—that is, if your Web site is to be merely a public-relations tool for a primarily offline business—then you can inexpensively and easily cobble together a simple Web site using software that you already own. Microsoft Word 2000 creates effective Web sites, for example, as does FrontPage 2000 (which comes free with some versions of Microsoft Office 2000). Almost every word-processing program these days saves in Web format (a.k.a. HTML), so you can create your pages just like regular word-processing documents and then convert them to Web pages with a simple Save As command.

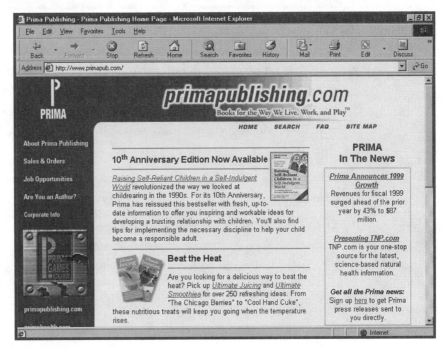

**Figure 4.4**

A professionally designed Web site instills confidence in the customer.

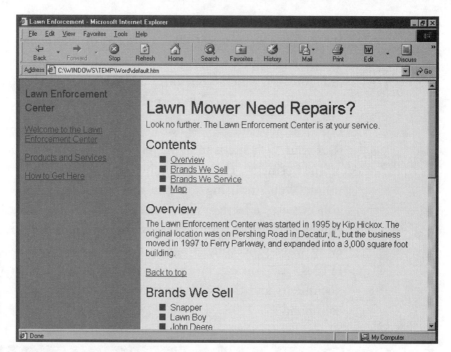

**Figure 4.5**

A home-made Web site conveys information, but the overall look and feel is amateurish.

Even if you plan to hire someone else to create your Web site, you should do a little bit of planning beforehand. You should go to the Web designer with a list of pages you want and a rough outline of the content to be included on each page. You should also have all the text that you want to include already written and have all the photos and artwork neatly organized.

Stuck for ideas as to what to put on your Web site? Here are some thought-starters:

○ Make the documentation for all the products you sell available online. You can make it available on regular Web pages, or use the PDF format to serve up publishing-quality pages suitable for printing.

- Offer a Frequently Asked Questions (and answers) page. This should cover the average person's most common inquiries about your product or service.

- Provide a map that shows how to get to your office (if you want customers to be able to find you physically, that is), along with directions from various parts of your city. You can link to a mapping site such as MapQuest (http://www.mapquest.com) for the map, create one with a drawing program, or scan one in as a graphic.

- List other Web sites that have information related to your products or services. For example, if you offer proofreading, you could provide links to sites with online dictionaries and writing style guides.

- Provide online ordering. You can do this through a shopping-cart system (in which visitors enter their shipping address and a credit card number), or more informally through e-mail. Many Web hosts provide a free shopping-cart system to use, although you might need to hire a Web designer to figure out how to use it most effectively.

- Allow customers to track their orders. If you have an online ordering system, you might want to expand it to allow customers to look up their status by order number, to find out whether an order has shipped.

## Marketing with E-mail

Almost everyone who has been online has received annoying junk e-mail, and most people make it a policy never to do business with anyone who would be so rude as to send an unsolicited advertisement like that. The last thing you want to do is anger potential customers, so you should never participate in blatant bulk e-mailing.

However, that doesn't mean you can't exploit e-mail for your business benefit. You can use e-mail for *marketing*, rather than advertising, to good effect. To do so, simply provide people something of value for free through e-mail. For example, you might create a mailing list of your customers' e-mail addresses, and send out a monthly message listing your current special discounts. Or you might create an e-mail newsletter with helpful stories and links to Web sites related to your product or service. Figure 4.6 shows an e-mail I recently received from a company called IPrint, for example, that offered me a special deal on printing.

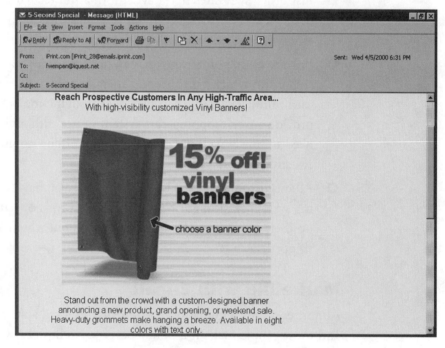

**Figure 4.6**

This e-mail is effective because it offers me something valuable—a discount.

E-mail mailings are most effective at good-will building when you follow these rules:

- **Don't e-mail indiscriminately.** Send your mailing only to people who have asked to receive it. You can include a sign-up form for your mailing list on your Web site, for example, or ask customers for their e-mail addresses when you complete a transaction.
- **Provide something of value.** Offer a special discount to readers of your e-mail. Provide free information about a product or service. Give people a reason to open your e-mail.
- **Don't mail too frequently.** Once or twice a month is plenty often.
- **Keep it short and to the point.** Don't ramble. Make sure the benefit is clear from the very first paragraph.

# For More Information

This chapter only scratched the surface of Internet use. There's much more to know about being an Internet user and an online content provider. Here are some other books that can teach you more:

**Create Your First Web Page In a Weekend** by Steve Callahan, 1999 Prima Communications Inc.

**Create FrontPage 2000 Web Pages In a Weekend** by C. Michael Woodward and Steve Callahan, 1999 Prima Communications Inc.

**Increase Your Web Traffic In a Weekend** by William Stanek, 2000 Prima Communications Inc.

**Customers.com: How to Create a Profitable Business Strategy for the Internet and Beyond** by Patricia Seybold, 1998 Random House, Inc.

**Marketing on the Internet** by Jan Zimmerman, 1999 Maximum Press

**Poor Richard's E-Mail Publishing** by Chris Pirillo, 1999 Top Floor Publishing.

**Poor Richard's E-Mail Marketing and Promotions** by Peter Kent and Tara Calishain, 1999 Top Floor Publishing

# Moving On...

Now you have a strategy for the connections you'll establish to the outside world from your home office. Whether it's telephone, faxing, or the Internet, you're ready to keep in touch.

In the Sunday morning session, I'll start you thinking about how you're going to get business. Will you advertise in print? Will you attend trade shows? Will you have a splashy ad in the Yellow Pages? Get a good night's sleep tonight, and face those questions in the A.M.

# Getting Business

- ✿ Developing a Business Plan
- ✿ Establishing Your Work Ethic
- ✿ Printed Materials That Say Who You Are
- ✿ Advertising: Let's Get Some Business!
- ✿ Marketing: Becoming a Household Name

**B**y now, if you don't have your office quite set up yet, you at least have a firm plan for completion. Maybe you even have the furniture and other equipment bought and paid for, and you're sitting in your ergonomic chair, looking at your tastefully decorated walls, lining up your pencils and paperclip holders just so, and thinking, "What now?"

For most people, the answer is "Get out there and get some business." The best equipped home office in the world can't help you if you don't have a sense of what your business practices should be, who you want for your customers, and how you'll find and retain those customers.

 **NOTE** If you're a telecommuter, or you already have all the clients you need, you can skip most of this session; just thumb through and read the parts that apply to your situation.

# Developing a Business Plan

You might be thinking at this point "My business is really simple; I don't need a business plan." But everyone can benefit from a business plan. Time spent thinking about your business practices is time well invested, even if you never need the actual document.

If you need to get financing for your business startup, you will need a well-written, neatly typed business plan. Lending institutions will use your business plan—along with your financial data such as your personal account balances and your debt ratio—to evaluate your loan-worthiness. At the minimum, make sure you spell-check your plan, print it on nice paper, and number the pages. If the business plan is just for your own purposes, it need not be quite so polished in format, but the same care should go into the ideas within.

A business plan is just what the name implies—a written plan for starting up and running the business. There is no one fixed format for a business plan, but most of them contain the sections that I'll describe in the next few pages.

## What Business Are You In?

This might seem like a no-brainer question, but it isn't. You need to define your business—to know what falls within its mission and what doesn't. For example, say you want to start a driveway-paving business. Good for you. Your business plan should describe the type of paving you will do (driveways), and whether you will do both residential and commercial work or residential only. It should discuss the area in which you will operate (for example, within a certain city and up to 50 miles outside of the city). It should distinguish your business from others by defining what you will and won't do. For example, perhaps you plan to pave driveways only with blacktop materials and not with concrete.

Think also about how you will deal with business offers that don't fall within your stated mission. For example, suppose you have your driveway-paving business up and running, and a neighbor asks whether you can put in a cement sidewalk in front of her house. Will you take this on? It's clearly outside of your stated business mission. If the answer is yes, perhaps you should revise your business mission now, so you'll feel free to take on a larger variety of assignments later as desired.

## What Is Your Long-Term Vision?

Don't be afraid to dream a little. Do you hope to someday turn your garage-based operation into a multimillion dollar company? (It's been done—lots of times.) Or do you hope to run the business as-is for 10 years and then retire? State your ultimate goal for the business.

## Who Are Your Customers?

When planning a business, it's important to know whom you'll be serving. It's tempting to leave it at "I'll serve anyone who will hire me," but that doesn't make for a well-focused business plan, nor a well-run business. You should know exactly who your customers will and won't be.

Continue with the driveway-paving example. Will your customers be owners of existing homes? Will you pave parking lots for businesses? Will you put in driveways for contractors building new houses? Make a list of all the potential customers that might be interested in your product or service, and then decide whom you want to serve.

You also need to figure out how your product or service is different from or better than what your customer base currently has. How will you convince customers to buy yours instead? For example, will your paving be of superior quality? Will it be more affordable? Will you offer faster service? Also, you need to state whom you will be competing with and what their product or service is like. What are its strengths and weaknesses? How can you make yours more appealing in comparison?

## How Will You Make Money?

If you are using the business plan as a tool to get a start-up loan, you'll need to be especially meticulous in preparing the financial section of your business plan.

For the Expenses section, list your startup costs, and explain why they're necessary. Then list the costs of day-to-day operation. If you plan to draw a salary from the business (otherwise how will you live?), state how much you need. For the Income section, list the sources of income and approximately how much you will receive from each source.

## What Do You Need to Do?

In order to achieve your goals, and in order to have a successful business, what needs to happen? Make a list of all the major tasks you will need to accomplish, and set a deadline for each one. For example, your list might include advertising, buying equipment, hiring an assistant, or making items to sell. Your plan should also state whether you are going to work at the business full-time or part-time and whether you will hire any consultants or experts to help you.

# Establishing Your Work Ethic

Everyone starts their business with the best of intentions, but, as the old cliché goes, "If you don't stand for something you'll fall for anything." In other words, if you don't establish firm policies and business ethics for yourself initially, it's too easy to make the wrong decision under stress.

## Motivating Yourself to Work

When you work in an office all day, your motivation is external. Your boss stops by to ask when certain projects will be completed, or your coworkers make it clear that they're counting on you to meet a deadline. But when you work at home, your motivation must be *internal*. Otherwise you'll find yourself watching talk shows all day.

The key to motivation is to figure out what motivates you, and then focus on it daily. The answer is different for different people, of course; here are some common motivators:

- **More money.** The harder you work, the more money you make. If you don't work, you don't earn.

- **Good reputation.** As an independent worker, you'll be judged on the work you do by clients. If you work hard and do a good job, you'll develop a strong reputation.

- **Greater satisfaction.** By doing well at your work, you'll be happier with yourself and have a better self image.

## Avoiding Procrastination

Remember at the beginning of this book, when I was talking about the pros and cons of home employment? One of the big pros—or cons, depending on your perspective—is that there's no supervisor to ride you until you get your work done. That means that if you decide to take the morning off and watch *Little House on the Prairie* reruns rather than work on a project that's due tomorrow, you won't get in trouble for it immediately.

However, it's a dangerous trap to fall into—to assume that because there are no immediate consequences for an action, that there will be no ultimate consequences. If you goof off instead of work, the work won't get done, and you'll ultimately lose a customer. So in the end, you're only hurting yourself. Coming to that realization now, rather than after you've lost some good customers, is the key to nipping procrastination in the bud.

One of my favorite sayings is "Discipline is remembering what you really want." What you really want is to have a successful business that will continue to provide profit and satisfaction for years to come and that will help you avoid having to work for someone else. You might think you want to sit in the sun this afternoon and read instead of do your work, but consider the ultimate outcome of that immediate desire, and it becomes much less attractive.

Here are some of my favorite strategies for overcoming procrastination:

❖ **Plan a reward for yourself.** After you've completed a task you've been dreading, splurge for a pound of the gourmet coffee you love, or take a 10-minute walk if it's a nice day.

❖ **Just start it.** Force yourself to get started. The task might not be as bad as you were anticipating.

❖ **Do the hard part first.** If there's an aspect of a project that you aren't looking forward to doing, do that part first to get it over with.

❖ **Don't allow yourself to get busy with less-important tasks.** For example, taking a half hour off to clip your dog's nails is fine normally, but if you're doing it to avoid your work, it's not fine.

❖ **Don't fall into the perfectionist trap.** Don't spend so much time perfecting one part of a project that you completely neglect another part (perhaps a part that you secretly didn't want to do, hmm?).

❖ **Schedule a day off.** If you're feeling burned out and overworked, schedule yourself an extra day off in the next week or so. Having relief in sight can help you find the focus for the task at hand.

❖ **Work should be enjoyable.** If you're procrastinating about some part of your work, it's probably because you don't enjoy that part. For the future, see whether there isn't a way you can hire out that part of the job, or avoid taking on projects that involve so much of it.

You've probably heard car salesmen with that old line, "What would it take for me to put you in this car today?" I use a variation of that to clear out the "can'ts" from my work schedule. If there's something I think I can't do, I ask myself, "What would it take to make it possible for you to do that?" For example, one time I was supposed to update a very technical article about laser printers. I had been putting it off because, frankly, I didn't know that much about them, and I was feeling intimidated. So I asked myself, "What would it take?" My internal dialog went like this:

"I would need to know more about the subject, to feel more comfortable writing about it."

"Okay, what would *that* take?"

"I would need to do some research, maybe on the Internet, and look at some other articles."

"And what would *that* take?"

"I could do that over my lunch hour today; I guess it wouldn't take that long. I could print some of them out and look at them this evening. Then I could write the article first thing tomorrow morning."

See how it worked? I just kept badgering myself with the "What would it take?" question until I came up with the solution.

## How Will You Derail Distractions?

Whereas procrastination is an internally driven demon that keeps you from your work, distractions are the externally driven equivalent.

The best way to avoid distraction is to know what distracts you. Are you tempted by daytime TV? Then don't walk into the room with the television until you're finished for the day. Does your family come into your office uninvited "just to say hi" or to get your opinion on trivial matters?

Try closing and locking your office door while you're working. In short, evaluate the situation and take the appropriate corrective measures.

Part of avoiding distraction is setting clear, reasonable boundaries. They'll be different for everyone, but here are some ideas:

- If you have children at home who need supervision, consider hiring a babysitter to be available while you are working so you won't be interrupted as frequently.

- Don't allow the boundary between work and home to be blurred by multitasking. For example, don't try to complete a rush job for a client and do laundry at the same time. Non-work responsibilities have a way of creeping in and eating up your work time.

- Define your office area in the home, and use that area only for work. Don't share a PC with the kids' games, for example, and don't work on personal correspondence at your work desk.

- If you find yourself easily distracted by outside stimuli, locate your office in a windowless room, or hang blinds or heavy curtains.

- Don't answer your home phone while you are working. Instead, get a reliable answering machine or voice mail system, and check your messages a few times a day, returning any important calls. Telemarketers will not usually leave a message.

- If a telemarketer does get through to you, interrupt their speech to say "Please remove this number from your list and don't call here again." Then hang up. Don't waste your time arguing.

- If you have a hard time distinguishing your work time from your home time, treat your home office as if it were a real corporate office. Get dressed to go to work, and leave the office only at lunchtime or during well-defined break periods.

- ✪ Maintain regular hours. Spend the same time every day in your office, whether or not you have work to do. If there's no work at the moment, use that time to read trade publications, search for freelance projects on the Internet, or polish your marketing materials.

- ✪ Don't play games on your work computer. Ever. Once you break this rule once, it's very hard to enforce it again.

## What Will Be Your Company Philosophy?

Every company needs a philosophy—a guiding principle or goal toward which it does business. For example, my primary goal as a freelance writer has been to build a good reputation in the publishing industry so that editors will request me for their projects. I have always figured that the money would come on its own if I simply focused on this philosophy, and it has.

Besides your overall philosophy statement, you should have definite plans for making that philosophy real. For example, here are some ways that I have set out to build my reputation as a writer:

- ✪ **Be pleasant to work with.** You'd be surprised how many egotistical, surly, litigious writers there are out there—and how many of them my poor beleaguered editors have worked with. Being accommodating and agreeable goes a long way toward getting future business.

- ✪ **Work for a fair wage.** Know what the going rates are in your industry, and don't insist on being paid more than everyone else. On the other hand, don't settle for less than the average either; you don't want to be known as "that person who will work for cheap."

- ✪ **Do outstanding work.** Do your utmost to make your product or service the very best available. This one is crucial.

○ **Offer extra value.** Whenever possible, give your customer a little extra. If your deadline is Tuesday, try to finish by Monday. If you've promised six hand-painted lawn gnomes, throw in a free wooden cart with the order.

○ **Be flexible to meet the customer's needs.** If your deadline is Tuesday, and the customer calls you on Saturday begging for you to work over the weekend, weigh the cost versus the benefit. If you do it, you might miss a party or two, but you'll have that customer's loyalty for years to come.

○ **Don't be afraid to negotiate.** If you feel like it's a big imposition on you to be asked to work over the weekend, politely negotiate for an incentive. If the customer needs the work done badly enough, he might be happy to pay you an extra 20% or more. But it won't occur to him to offer it unless you ask.

## How Will You Handle Problems?

Your business needs a firm policy for dealing fairly with your customers. Knowing what you'll do in a given situation and having it planned out in advance can save you from making a spur-of-the-moment bad decision.

Many successful businesses work on the principle that the customer is always right. That doesn't actually mean that the customer is really right in every dispute; it simply means that you must do whatever you can to make the customer satisfied. Satisfied customers, after all, are customers who'll be back the next time they need your product or service. A customer who feels wronged will not only never do business with you again but will probably tell several other people about his dissatisfaction. As restaurateurs will tell you, it is often a much better investment to give away a dessert or two than it is to lose a regular customer.

What will you do in each of the following situations?

- **Defective product return**. If a product is defective, how will you proceed? Will you repair the product, or replace it? What warranty will you offer—30 days? One year? Longer?

- **Non-defective product return**. Within how many days can a non-defective product be returned? Is a receipt needed for a cash refund? Will there be a restocking fee?

- **Service refund**. If the customer is not happy with your service, how will you make it right? Will you redo the job for free? What if it's the customer's fault that the job needs to be redone? How will you make that determination?

- **Lateness**. If you provide a product or service later than you promised, how will you compensate? Will you give the customer a discount? Will you throw in a free product or service? Or will you do nothing unless the customer complains?

# Take a Break

I'll bet you weren't expecting to do all this planning and strategizing as part of your home office setup, eh? Most people get so wrapped up in what computer to buy and what color to paint the walls that they forget that the most important part of the business is the brain of the person who runs it.

But take a break from all this thinking for a moment, and enjoy a cup of coffee. Better yet, turn your brain off completely for a while and watch a *Gilligan's Island* rerun or some MTV videos. Then return refreshed and ready for more. The rest of this session continues to help you plan your business by helping you create a corporate image.

# Printed Materials That Say Who You Are

Neale Donald Walsch, one of my favorite authors, writes that "Every act is an act of self-definition." In other words, everything you do or say helps define who you are and who you want to be. This is true in business as well as in personal dealings.

Most businesses need printed items, such as business cards, stationery, envelopes, and so on. Because these items go out to customers and vendors, they make a strong statement about the company. Therefore it's important that you choose the right design, the right paper, and the right printing, to make sure they convey your business's message accurately.

When I say stationery, I don't mean the flowered note cards that the term usually conjures up. Stationery in a business sense consists of 8.5×11 sheets of paper with your return address (and perhaps other information) already printed on it, along with matching business-size envelopes.

Your business cards, your stationery, and your other items should share a common look and feel. That means you need to decide on a color scheme, a logo, and a typeface up front, and make sure they are consistently applied in all your printed materials.

## Color Scheme

The cheapest way to print is to use a single color only. Most printing places don't charge extra for a single color other than black (or charge only a little bit extra), so you might consider brown, dark blue, or dark green ink instead. Avoid using a bright single color such as bright red; it limits readability. And avoid purple (for most industries) as it has a too-casual feel. You can achieve some surprisingly nice effects with a single ink color and some colored and/or textured paper.

If you have the budget for it, consider a corporate color scheme (that is, two or more colors that you will use repeatedly in all your materials). The colors you choose depend on the message you want to send to your customers. Bright, primary colors like red and blue say simplicity and clarity. Dark shades like dark green and cranberry say sophistication and subtlety. Black and yellow are evocative of construction and manufacturing; browns and oranges say warmth. You get the idea.

# Logo

A *logo* is a symbol or simple graphic that represents your company. It can appear along with the company name or as a substitute for it. You don't absolutely have to have a logo, but it makes your printed materials look nicer to have some sort of graphic.

Don't make the mistake of getting too detailed and complex with your graphic. Too many details and fine lines make it hard to reproduce and hard to recognize. Stick with big shapes and simple lines.

No ideas spring to mind? Try combining the first letter or the initials of the business name with some simple shapes such as ovals, rectangles, or triangles. Experiment on paper or in a computer-graphics program. Figure 5.1 shows an example.

**Figure 5.1**

A simple logo, created with the WordArt feature of Microsoft Word

Once you get the basic design, you might want to hire a professional graphic designer to polish and clean up your logo.

## Font

*Font* is another name for typeface. The font you choose for your printed materials conveys the personality of the business. Do you want to be perceived as whimsical? Serious? Refined? Bold? The font you choose can make the difference.

Consider the examples shown in the next section. It's the same business card, but with four different fonts—and four different personalities.

The fonts you can choose from depend on where you have your printing done. If you print your own materials from your own PC, you can use whatever fonts are installed on your system. If you use a commercial printing service, you're limited to the fonts they have.

## Business Cards

Business cards used to be rather boring and standardized. The company name and logo would be on a white card, with the name, title, and contact information of the person to whom the card belonged. Yawn.

Nowadays, however, it's quite a different story. You can have full-color business cards with photographic backgrounds, custom-cut cards with holes punched out of the middle, bright full-color graphics, and any number of other eye-catching variations on the traditional business card. Figure 5.2 shows some examples.

**Figure 5.2**

The font can make a big difference in a business card. These were created in Microsoft Publisher 2000.

Here are the decisions you need to make when selecting business cards:

- **Cost.** How much are you willing to spend? If you want functionality on a tight budget, print your own cards on your PC's printer, or have single-color cards printed up at a local copy center.

- **Purpose.** What role will business cards serve in your business? If you are continually out there glad-handing for new clients, great business cards are a must; if you'll spend most of your time in the office, perhaps not.

- **Type.** Do you want a plain cardstock with printing? Or would you prefer a shiny photographic card, or a card with a hologram, or punched-out areas, or some odd shape? Keep in mind that the more unusual the design, the more it'll cost.

- **Portrait or landscape.** Will the writing run across the narrow edge of the card, or the wide? Traditional business cards are landscape (that is, wider than they are tall); however, some people prefer the more unusual, eye-catching portrait orientation.

- **Paper.** Will you use white cardstock, or some other color? Will it be a matte finish or a glossy one? How thick will the paper be? Ask to see some paper samples if you are unsure (if buying locally).

- **Where to buy them.** If business cards will be important to your business, I urge you to have them professionally done rather than printing them up yourself at home. Your local copy shop might provide business-card printing; you can also get good-quality cards inexpensively from online vendors.

**NOTE**   iPrint.com is a company that lets you design your own business cards on their Web site, then order them online. You receive your cards by mail in a week or so. You can find them at http://www.iprint.com.

## Stationery

If you will be writing letters to customers, already printed stationery will lend a professional touch to the correspondence. Your stationery should match your business cards in color scheme, logo, and font choices.

Typical business stationery includes the complete company address, as well as phone number, Web site address, and any other contact information available. This information is traditionally presented at the top, although it can also be on the bottom or at the left for a change of pace from the ordinary. You might also want some sort of graphic line or divider to separate the information from the body of the letter.

What to put on your stationery? Well, at the minimum, your return address. But you can also use your stationery to show off your credentials or to tell what your business does. Figure 5.3 shows a couple examples.

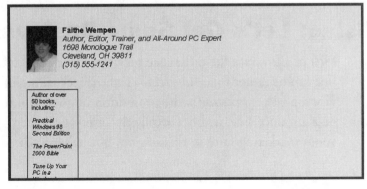
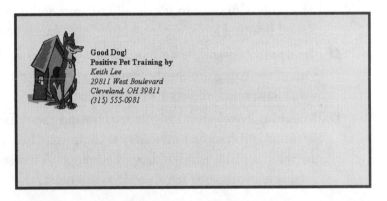

**Figure 5.3**

Two letterhead examples with varying amounts of information

Some people use a business name rather than their own name on stationery and business cards, even when the company consists of only a single freelancer. That's up to you. Think about who your customers will be and whether they would find more value in dealing personally with you as an expert or in dealing with a company.

Here's what to look for in business stationery:

- **Paper.** Choose a neutral color (white, cream, light gray, or light tan), and make sure it's a heavy, good-quality stock (at least 20lb). Many experts say that off-white is the best color for business stationery because then the reader doesn't notice the color. Textured paper is nice, but is more expensive and sometimes doesn't work well in printers.

- **Printing.** The same rules for fonts apply for stationery as for business cards. Choose a font carefully to portray the image you want. Raised printing looks expensive and fancy, but it costs more.

- **Text positioning.** Use no more than two inches at the top and bottom of the page combined for your preprinted text. Otherwise you won't have much room to write your letters!

- **Matching envelopes.** I highly recommend these. The effect of your beautiful, professional stationery is completely lost if your letter arrives in a plain, hand-addressed envelope. A matching envelope preprinted with your return address is a must.

# Advertising: Let's Get Some Business!

First of all, what's the difference between advertising and marketing? The line can be rather fine. *Advertising* is the direct selling of a product or service for sale; *marketing* is the promotion of good will toward a company or a product line without explicitly offering an item for sale. I'll talk about marketing later in this session, but let's look at advertising now.

# Print Publications

Even if you live in a very small town, you probably have a local newspaper or magazine. Pick up a copy, and notice how many businesses advertise there. Obviously, print advertising must be working for these other local businesses, or they wouldn't continue to pay for it. Will it work for you too? That depends on the nature of your business and the quality of the ad you develop.

A publication will want a *camera-ready* ad—that is, one that is already set up in the correct format, with all the pictures in place, ready to print. You can develop one on your own PC using a program like Microsoft Publisher. First, find out the rates and sizes for the publication. For example, you might be able to place a 3×4-inch ad for $100 in a small-circulation newspaper. Then design your ad to be exactly the size you want. Figure 5.4 shows a sample camera-ready ad.

CAUTION

◆◆◆◆◆◆◆◆◆◆◆◆◆◆◆◆◆◆◆◆◆◆◆◆◆◆◆◆◆◆◆◆◆◆◆◆◆◆◆◆◆◆

Remember that newspapers are in black-and-white, so don't create an ad that relies on color for a newspaper.

◆◆◆◆◆◆◆◆◆◆◆◆◆◆◆◆◆◆◆◆◆◆◆◆◆◆◆◆◆◆◆◆◆◆◆◆◆◆◆◆◆◆

**Figure 5.4**

A camera-ready ad for a print publication

The format you submit your ad in depends on the publication and its preferences. Some publications accept only hard-copy ads; others accept computer disks containing data files in certain formats. If the program you use to create the ad can save in a variety of file formats, check with the publication staff to find out which of your available formats they can accept.

**TIP**

You can get free publicity in local publications by submitting articles and press releases; see "Free Publicity in Local Papers" later in this session for details.

Running a coupon in your ad is a great way to generate business. People might throw away a normal ad, but they will clip and save a coupon if they think there's a possibility they might want the item or service. Think about it—isn't that exactly what you do yourself? Figure 5.5 shows a sample coupon.

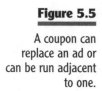

**Figure 5.5**

A coupon can replace an ad or can be run adjacent to one.

PC Diagnostic Software

**FREE**

With any service call
Burrow PC Repair Services
Tel: 555-981-8271
Expiration Date:    12/01/01

# Internet Ads

If your customers are predominantly Internet users, consider running an Internet ad. (Most noncomputer businesses won't benefit that much from Internet advertising.)

An Internet ad is a little different from a regular ad in that the primary purpose of the ad is not to get the user to call you and place an order. Instead, the purpose of an ad is to get the user to click on the ad. When the user clicks on the ad, your Web page appears, and from there, the object is to get the person to place an order. It goes without saying, therefore, that you must have a Web site to link to in order to benefit from Internet advertising; you learned about Web sites in the Saturday evening session.

Therefore, an Internet ad does not need to tell the whole story. It doesn't even have to include your company name and contact information. Its only purpose is to intrigue people enough that they want to click on it to get more information.

The standard Internet ad size is a banner. A banner is 468 pixels wide by 60 pixels tall. Ads are measured online in pixels rather than in inches because the actual size of the ad depends on the size of monitor on which it is viewed. A pixel is an individual dot that makes up the display. Figure 5.6 shows a typical banner ad. This one is nothing fancy; you'll see much better ads online. It's just a simple text ad I made up in Paint Shop Pro to show you the approximate size and shape needed.

**Figure 5.6**

A banner ad for use on a Web page

> **Get Healthy Now!**
> **Free Vitamin Samples...click here**

You can create a banner ad in any computer-graphics program, such as Paint Shop Pro, Photoshop, or whatever you happen to have. (You can get a free trial version of Paint Shop Pro from http://www.jasc.com.) Make sure you create a new file that's exactly the right number of pixels in size, and then just fill the canvas with whatever you want on your banner. Save it in GIF or JPEG format, and provide it to the Web sites on which you buy advertising.

A banner ad can consist of two or more separate images that alternate. This movement from one image to another attracts the customer's attention, and also gives you more space to provide your message. For example, you might alternate between the following two banners shown in Figure 5.7. To create an animated ad like this, you will need a graphics program that can create animated GIF files. Paint Shop Pro has an add-on program that can do this, as do many other graphics programs; alternatively, you can hire a computer-graphics professional to create the ad for you.

**NOTE**

As you can see from Figures 5.5 and 5.6, the average non-Web-design professional (such as me!) turns out rather amateurish-looking banner ads. To compete with the sophisticated advertising campaigns on the Internet these days, you should consider hiring a Web-design professional to help you with your ads if banner advertising on the Internet will be an important part of your business.

**Figure 5.7**

These two banners alternate on the screen, creating a moving ad.

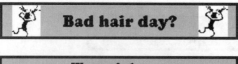

Bad hair day?

We can help.
Hair Designs by Kenneth. 555-7175

You can also advertise via e-mail, as I mentioned in last night's session, but you need to be careful to observe Internet etiquette or you might do more harm than good to your company. Make sure you send something of value to each recipient, such as a special offer, and make sure you send e-mail only to people who have requested it (such as those who have signed up for your mailing list).

## Radio and TV Ads

Most people immediately dismiss radio and TV as advertising media because of the cost. But if you advertise in smaller markets, the cost can actually be rather reasonable. I worked for a computer-training business that shot a 30-second commercial for about $600, and then paid about $1,000 to run it eight times on a local cable TV channel.

With a radio or TV ad spot, a lot of the cost comes from creating the ad. For radio, you'll need to hire professional voice talent and rent a recording studio. For TV, you'll need a camera operator, some actors, some lights, and a director who knows about shooting commercials.

Fortunately, you're not completely on your own. Your local radio and TV or cable operators want you to create ads, so they often provide assistance. Perhaps your local radio station will let you hire one of its deejays to record your ad and will let you use its studio and equipment, in exchange for a commitment to run the ad a certain number of times. Or perhaps your local cable TV company will rent you a cameraman and director to help you develop your commercial.

Another way to find out what's available in your area is to ask the owner of another local business who is already advertising where you want to be. Find out how he or she created the ad and how much it cost.

# Marketing: Becoming a Household Name

Marketing is the generation of name recognition and good will. Marketing helps a brand name such as Levi's or Kleenex become so famous that it's virtually synonymous with the product class. Marketing keeps your company's name and product in the backs of people's minds, so that the next time they need your product or service, yours is the name that occurs to them immediately.

Unlike regular advertising, marketing does not necessarily promote a single product or service. Therefore, you don't always have to pay for marketing; a lot of great marketing happens under the guise of public information. You'll see some examples in the following sections.

## Free Publicity in Local Papers

How would you like to have a whole page of free publicity in a local publication? Yes, it's possible, and it's really easy to get, too. Just write an article about yourself and your business. Most small publications are hungry for local-interest stories and will snap up any contributions they receive.

For example, suppose your business is furniture refinishing, and you have been hired by a local church to refinish its pews. Get together with the church staff, and find out a little about the history of the church—such as where the pews came from, when the church was built, that sort of thing. Then write up a feature about how you will be helping beautify this historical site and include lots of details about the restoration process. Any small-town editor will be profusely grateful for a free story, and everyone in town will read about your business. It's a win-win. If you can't write very well, hire someone to write the story for you—a local journalism student, for example, or a high-school niece or nephew. Your cost will be less than the cost of a much smaller ad.

You need not write a long article; a single paragraph can also be effective. Here's an example of a short, simple press release:

---

### LOCAL CRAFTSMAN TO RESTORE HISTORIC CHURCH

The First United Methodist Church of Okansaw, long known for its beautiful carved wood ornamentation, has selected Tom Benson to manage the restoration of its pews this summer. The First United Methodist Church of Okansaw was originally built in 1892, and the current pews were installed in 1921. "I am excited to be working on such lovely historic pieces," reports Tom Benson, "and I look forward to putting my many years of wood-refinishing experience to work for such a good cause." Mr. Benson owns Benson Refinishing, a local business specializing in the restoration of fine antique wood.

---

This doesn't have to be a one-time thing, either. Any time you win an award, give a speech, attend a convention, launch a Web site, or anything else out of the ordinary, send a press release. If it's a slow news day (or week), you just might end up in print for free.

**TIP** Make sure you always have a current photo of yourself handy, or a photo of your business or your product if that's more appropriate for your industry. Then submit a copy of the photo whenever you submit an article or press release.

## Local Professional Organizations

As a business owner, you want to establish yourself as a leader in your field. One great way to do that is to participate in local organizations related to your profession. For example, if you are a computer technician, join your area's computer society or club. If possible, serve in a leadership position in that club. Yes, it'll take up some of your time, but it'll also set you up as an expert in the eyes of other club members. And as a leader, you can legitimately issue press releases on behalf of the organization that include your name and a quote from you. More free self-promotion! Don't feel bad in the least about self-promotion; it works.

As a club member, try to encourage public outreach events. Any time you deal with the public, you're further establishing yourself with more potential customers. For example, if you're a computer technician, convince the computer club that it's a great idea to hold a free Internet seminar at a local retirement center, helping seniors buy and set up their own PCs. Then pass out your business card to each new PC owner. Chances are good that most of them will need a technician eventually, and most people would rather work with someone they already know (maybe that nice young man who helped them set the PC up for free).

## Free Seminars

Even if there aren't any other people in your area with which to form a professional organization, you can still do community outreach. Offering a free seminar is one of the best ways to get new customers.

Advertise your seminar in the local newspaper, or put up flyers around your area of town. You can invite people to your home or rent a facility, whichever fits your needs better. Give a free lecture on your subject of expertise—two hours is about right—with refreshments. If you have items to sell, have them readily available to buy on site, but don't push. Then pass out your business cards (and brochures if you have them), shake everyone's hand, and wait. Within a few weeks, you should have some new customers.

Don't be disappointed if you don't get good attendance at your seminar. The advertising you placed for it will still pay off indirectly. If you offer regular seminars and advertise each one in advance, you'll soon be known as "that person who does those seminars on [*your subject*]," and the next time anyone needs your product or service, your name will spring to mind.

## Donations and Sponsorships

Most cities and town have all kinds of marketing opportunities disguised as community events. A local museum might have a chili cook-off in which your business could sponsor a booth. A church's fundraiser for its new organ might need donations for its silent auction. Opportunities to promote yourself and your business are everywhere. These are win-win because

○ They typically don't cost much.

○ They build lots of good will.

○ There typically aren't a lot of other advertisers, so your ad gets noticed more than in a newspaper or magazine.

For example, suppose your daughter's high school is putting on a play. Your business could donate a couple of hundred dollars in exchange for a half-page "sponsored by" notice in the program. Now, every parent in town is going to be at that play, and they're all going to get there early and have nothing to do except read that program. And there's your sponsorship, prominently displayed. That's good marketing! Because now all the parents know about your business, and know that you're a civic-minded individual who cares about their kids' play.

## Pens, Mugs, and Other Giveaways

Big companies spend millions of dollars each year to set up splashy booths at trade shows and give away free merchandise with their logo on it. You can do the same thing, only on a much smaller scale.

Here's a human-nature tip: People will not throw away anything that's useful, even if it's a blatant piece of advertising. When you print your company name on a pen or mug and give it away, you've just injected your company name into that person's life for the lifespan of the item. Every day the person uses that pen or mug, he sees your company's name.

This kind of marketing really works. I've got all kinds of stuff I've picked up at trade shows—an insulated six-pack cooler from Aquanta, a mouse pad from IBM, a computer toolkit from KCR. I still use the items, and I still remember the names of the companies because I see their logos frequently.

Where do you get this stuff? There are all kinds of companies that offer personalized business printing on promotional items. You can get it at iPrint, for example, at http://www.iprint.com. Or look in your local Yellow Pages for a local supplier. Items are available for every budget; you can pay as little as 30¢ for an ink pen, or as much as $200 or more for a jacket with your company logo stitched on the back.

## Sponsoring Contests and Sweepstakes

Have you ever thought about *why* a company offers a contest or sweepstakes? No, it's not because they enjoy giving away big prizes for no reason. It's because a contest or sweepstakes makes good business sense.

What do you get when you hold a contest or sweepstakes? Two things. First of all, you get marketing recognition. People read your company's name in the rules, and then they write your company's name on their entry envelope. Second, You get *names and addresses*—people to whom you can send your mailings and promotions. Some companies pay big bucks to buy mailing lists, but when you hold a give-away, consumers willingly give you their contact information for free!

A *contest* is judged according to the quality of the entries. For example, you might have an essay contest in which participants are to write 100 words or less about why they want to win whatever it is you're giving away. In some states you can charge money to enter a contest; in others you can't. (But if your primary purpose is to build good will and get a lot of names and addresses, you probably won't want to charge for entry.)

In contrast, a *sweepstakes* is a luck-of-the-draw event in which you select a winner at random. Sweepstakes are, by definition, free to enter. You can require a proof-of-purchase, but there must be some alternative free way of entering too.

**NOTE** Don't confuse sweepstakes with raffles or lotteries. These latter two require people to buy a ticket, and in most states it's illegal for an individual or business to hold a for-profit raffle or lottery. Some charities are exempt in some areas; check your local regulations.

Every state has its own mind-bogglingly complex regulations for contests and sweepstakes, so you'll need to make sure yours complies. About.com has a couple of very useful articles online about setting up a sweepstakes. You can find them at http://contests.about.com. Another source: Arent Fox Attorneys at Law provide a lot of legal information about sweepstakes and contests at their Web site, http://www.arentfox.com.

The information in these articles, while very useful, is no substitute for personalized legal advice. If you plan to sponsor a contest or sweepstakes, consult an attorney to make sure you don't run afoul of the very complex laws governing them.

# Moving On...

At this point you should have some ideas about how you plan to attract and retain your customers. You should have at least started your business plan, and know what you want to order in terms of business cards and stationery. You should also understand your options for advertising and marketing, and have some ideas of what promotions would be effective for your business.

One more chapter to go! In this afternoon's session, I'll get into the nitty-gritty details of keeping a business running and keeping yourself financially solvent as an entrepreneur.

# Finances and Record Keeping

When I first started my business, the financial aspect seemed very intimidating. I had tried to study accounting many years ago, but the whole double-entry thing confused the heck out of me. Ledgers, journals, accounts receivable—I had no idea where to start.

I eventually figured it all out on my own, but you shouldn't have to. In this final session, I'll pass on some of what I've learned over the years about small business accounting, taxes, insurance, and retirement planning.

## Doing Business As...

For financial and legal purposes, you must decide whether you'll have a business name or simply use your own name. If you have a business name, that's your DBA—your "Doing Business As" name. For example, John Smith DBA *The Plumbing Guy.*

The decision of whether to use your own name might be made for you, depending on some of your other choices. Do you plan to incorporate your business, or are you going to remain a sole proprietor? As a sole proprietor, you'll file your taxes under your own name, so a business name is optional. But if you set up a corporation or partnership, you will need a business name to differentiate the company from your personal self both

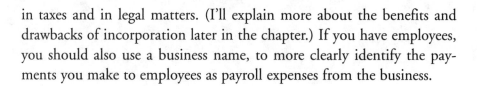

in taxes and in legal matters. (I'll explain more about the benefits and drawbacks of incorporation later in the chapter.) If you have employees, you should also use a business name, to more clearly identify the payments you make to employees as payroll expenses from the business.

# Small Business Banking

You're not going to store all that money under your mattress, are you? I thought not. So you'll need a bank account or two.

# Can I Use My Existing Checking Account?

A lot of home workers start out using their existing personal checking accounts for their business income. The advantages: no extra monthly fees and easy access to a single pool of money. If you have only one or two clients, or perhaps are a telecommuter, this can work, but it's not the best way of doing business, because

- ✿ If you have other sources of income besides income from your business, or if you have two or more separate businesses, record keeping will be difficult if you try to share a single bank account for all purposes. When your bank statement comes each month, you'll have to figure out which expenses are for what.

- ✿ Most small-business accounting programs assume that you will have one or more bank accounts exclusively for the business. You won't be able to get the most out of your accounting program if you don't have separate business and personal accounts.

- ✿ If customers make out their checks to your business's name instead of to you personally, you might have some trouble depositing them into your personal account. With a business account, you can set up a DBA name, and you can deposit checks made out to either your name or your business's name.

- ✿ If you later need to apply for a bank loan, you will need to clearly distinguish your business finances from your personal ones. It will help if you have several months of bank statements from a business-only account. Lenders will think you aren't serious about your business if you don't have a separate bank account for it.

- ✿ When filling out your taxes at the end of the year, it'll be much easier to distinguish business from personal expenses if the money is separate. For example, the bank fees for a business checking account are fully deductible, but the bank fees for personal checking are not.

- ✿ If the IRS ever audits you, it will help greatly in proving your income and expenses to have your business finances separate from your personal ones, especially if your personal account is shared with someone else.

To sum it all up: A business bank account is a good investment—even with the extra costs it entails.

## Selecting a Bank

Whether you decide to go with a business account or a personal one, shop around. Find a bank that offers good services at a reasonable fee, and a bank with a branch with hours that are convenient for you. I chose my bank, for example, because it has a branch in the grocery store where I shop. This branch is open late every evening and all day on Saturday, so I don't have to plan my trips to the bank around limited hours like with some institutions. Even though it's not the cheapest bank in terms of monthly fees, the extra convenience is worth it to me.

**TIP**
You might want to consider banking at a credit union. These institutions are member-owned. Credit unions do not have to pay stock dividends, so their fees are usually lower. Many larger credit unions have ATM networks, branches, and similar services to other banks. A growing number of companies, unions, state and local governments, and communities have established credit unions that you might be eligible to join. If one member qualifies, usually everyone in the family can join. Credit unions are federally insured, like other credible banks.

Here are some questions to ask yourself when evaluating various banks:

- How many checks will you write per month, and how many deposits will you make? Does the bank offer an account that fits well with the banking volume you expect to conduct?

- What minimum and average balance do you think you will have in the account? Does the bank offer an account that's a good deal given your balance estimate?

- What additional services do you think you might need, such as letters of credit, payroll services, loans, or bill payment? Does the bank offer any special deals on these services for account holders?

- What time of day is most convenient for you to go to the bank? Is the bank open at that time?

- Do you prefer dealing with a live teller or an ATM machine? Does the bank provide your preferred method for free, or is there a fee associated?

- Does the bank have an ATM convenient to your home? If you have to use some other bank's ATM, how much in fees do you estimate you will rack up per month?

- Do you prefer to have all your financial services in the same place, or would you rather find the best deal for each service individually (checking, savings, loans, and so on)?

# Online Banking

Online banks (a.k.a. virtual banks) exist only on the Web, so their fees are often much lower (and interest rates higher) than banks that have to maintain branch locations. You can also get detailed information about your account online, 24 hours a day.

I had an online bank account for a while, but closed it after about six months. Why? Several reasons:

✪ **ATM fees.** Because the bank didn't have any local ATM machines, I had to pay $1.50 every time I withdrew cash at an ATM.

✪ **Deposit hassles.** I had to mail my deposits to the bank, so there was at least a three-day delay between when I received a check from a client and when I had access to the money. I also felt insecure about mailing endorsed checks.

✪ **Poor customer service.** Whenever I needed to call for help with the account, the people I talked to didn't understand the system very well, and on one particularly ghastly afternoon I got bounced around to seven different operators before someone could answer my question.

**NOTE**  If you want to pay bills online, but don't want to open an online banking account, online bill-paying services offer another virtual solution. These services allow you to receive your bills electronically instead of by mail. Each time a new bill comes in, you receive an e-mail telling you that a new bill is ready to be viewed. You review the bill online, select a payment date, and authorize a payment amount. These services generally cost $7 to $9 a month.

# Selecting a Bank Account Type

As if choosing a financial institution weren't mind-boggling enough, once you get there you'll probably have your choice of several account types.

## Personal Account

The banks in my area offer very good deals for personal checking accounts, with no fees, free ATM cards, free checks, and all kinds of other perks. Unfortunately, they don't usually offer any bargains whatsoever for business accounts. I pay about $15 a month for my business checking account; the fees in your area might vary somewhat.

One possible solution is to set up a separate personal checking account for your business under your own name. This can cost less per month than a business account, depending on the deal you get. However, there are some drawbacks:

- You might not be able to cash checks made out to your business rather than to you personally.

- The fact that it's a personal account without the business's name on it might not sit well with lenders if you ever need to borrow money.

- You won't have access to any special services the bank provides for small businesses, such as a business line of credit or a low-interest business credit card.

## Basic Business Account

If you don't write a lot of checks per month and don't need any special services, a "no frills" business account might be best for you. It's for customers who use the account primarily to pay bills and make deposits and don't maintain a high balance.

### Interest-Bearing Checking

If you typically maintain a high balance, consider an interest-bearing account. These usually have some minimum amount (such as $1,000 or higher) required to avoid paying fees. If your balance stays above the prescribed amount, you earn monthly interest. This type of account is sometimes restricted to sole proprietorships, nonprofit organizations, or government agencies.

### Package of Business Services

If you need lots of banking services, you might be able to get a good deal on a package from a bank. Your package might include, for example, a checking account, a savings account, banking by phone, banking by Internet, a business line of credit, and/or merchant credit-card services.

## Keeping Banking Costs Low

No matter where you choose to bank, you can manage your costs by being aware of what services are subject to an additional fee and minimizing your use of them.

Here are some of the services you might need that you could be charged for:

- Using an ATM
- Balance inquiries at an ATM
- Seeing a teller in person
- Writing a check
- Overdraft protection
- Going below minimum balance
- Bouncing a check
- Using another bank's ATM

- Placing stop payments on checks
- Getting canceled checks each month
- Closing your account
- Monthly processing

Some banks charge for the above items only in certain circumstances—for example, at my bank, if I maintain a balance of $3,000 in my business account, all services are free. Other banks allow you to have linked accounts, so that the balance maintained in one account (for example, savings) allows you to avoid the fees on another account (for example, checking).

Using direct deposit can also save you money. Some banks offer to waive certain fees if you use direct deposit because it saves them money not having to process paper checks.

# Home Office Record Keeping

As the owner of your business, you're responsible only to yourself, right? Wrong. You're also responsible to the IRS. You must keep accurate records so that you'll know how much tax to pay—and so you can prove that you have paid enough taxes in the event of an audit.

When it's just you, and you have to choose between entering last week's receipts into your accounting software and working on this week's jobs, it's easy to let your accounting duties fall by the wayside. But it's also dangerous to the health of your business. By not entering all your income, you're setting yourself up for tax underpayment. By not entering all your expenses, you're cheating yourself out of potential tax deductions. Even if you plan to update your records soon, a week can become a month, and a month can become a quarter, and pretty soon it's tax time and you're staring blankly at a pile of receipts and invoices that you can't remember why you saved.

# Choosing Accounting Software

If you have a good accounting background, it's possible to keep your own books on paper in ledgers you can buy at any office-supply store. But it's certainly not my preference! Not when accounting software is so inexpensive and so easy to use. You can save literally hundreds of hours per year by automating your accounting on your computer.

The top two contenders are QuickBooks and Peachtree Complete. QuickBooks is probably the better choice for a single-employee sole proprietorship because it's easier to learn and more intuitive to use. Peachtree Complete, on the other hand, might be a better choice for a larger small business with a real office and several employees. If you're reading this book, QuickBooks is probably what you want.

QuickBooks comes in two flavors: regular (about $70) and Pro (about $150). The Pro version comes with these additional features that the regular version lacks:

- Job cost estimating tools
- Time tracking
- Integration with contact info from Outlook or Act
- Integration with Microsoft Word and Excel
- Progress invoicing

If you don't need any of those features, go with the standard version because it's much cheaper.

If you have never used an accounting program such as QuickBooks before, you're in for a shock at how much the program can do. It manages your business bank accounts, prints invoices and purchase orders, generates reports, connects to the Internet for updates and bill-paying, and lots more. Figure 6.1 shows a sample screen from QuickBooks.

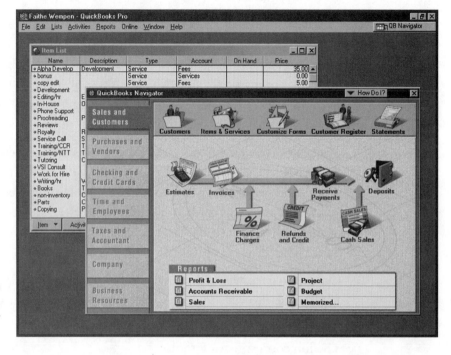

**Figure 6.1**

QuickBooks helps
you manage your
business finances.

If your financial recording needs are very simple, you don't even need QuickBooks. You
can get by on a program designed for home financial records, like Quicken or Microsoft
Money.

# What Records Should I Keep?

If you use a business-accounting computer program to manage your
finances, most of the records you need to keep will be automatically
stored in the program. (Make sure you back up your data file frequently,
so you won't lose these valuable business records if your computer has
problems.)

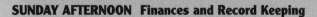

For example, when you use QuickBooks to create an invoice for a new customer, it stores the customer's name and address in its database and generates an entry in your Accounts Receivable ledger. Then when you receive the payment, you enter it in QuickBooks and it records the deposit in your business checking account, marks the invoice as paid, and updates that customer's payment history record.

If you don't use an accounting program, you will need to keep all your records on paper. At the bare minimum, you will need a general ledger (kind of like a detailed checkbook register), listing all the income and expenses.

What about paper items to save? Well, you need to save the receipts for all of your expenses so you can deduct them on your taxes. (You'll also enter all these expenses individually in your accounting program, but you'll need the proof in the form of actual receipts if you are ever audited.)

If you use paper invoices instead of computer-generated ones, you will also want to keep copies of all the invoices you issue. At an office supply store, you can get invoice books that produce carbon copies of each invoice you write. This serves as written proof of your income.

Finally, if clients send you statements of the money they have paid you (such as a 1099-MISC form), you will need to save those for reference when you are filling out your taxes for the year. I keep mine with my tax return copies for the year in which they were issued.

# Protecting Your Intellectual Property

Intellectual property consists of trademarks, inventions, designs, logos, and other items that define your business. When you first start out, you think that nobody would want to be associated with your business, but as you become more successful, imitators will invariably crop up to infringe on your rights.

So what kind of property do you own that you want to protect? Here are some examples:

- **Distinguishable product identifiers.** Words, phrases, or emblems that identify a particular product. An example of these would be Kleenex or Xerox.

- **Inventions.** Innovations that solve specific problems or improve technology and can be industrially manufactured. Examples of inventions might be a new metal cutting device or an engine component to improve oil stability.

- **Designs.** Innovations that illustrate how to manufacture an invention. Designs can be blueprints, engineering specifications, or computer drawings. Designs also are patented.

- **Original works of authorship.** Literary works, graphics, software, architectural works, photographs, music, audiovisuals, and sculptures. An example might be a new software program to better identify inventory or a composition of music.

## What Protection Do You Need?

Once you have determined the type of intellectual property you own, you next decide what type of protective vehicle is best suited for you. There are three applications available from the U.S. Patent and Trademark Office (PTO) for protecting your property:

- **Patent.** A *patent* is a document describing an invention or design. It creates a legal situation in which the patented invention can be used only under the authorization of the patent holder.

- **Copyright.** A *copyright* is the registration of original literary, artistic, photographic, software, musical, audiovisual, dramatic, or sculptural work. When you create a work, you automatically hold the copyright for it. However, registering your copyright protects

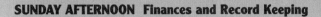 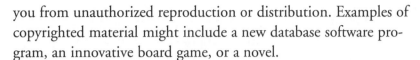

you from unauthorized reproduction or distribution. Examples of copyrighted material might include a new database software program, an innovative board game, or a novel.

✪  **Trademark.** A *trademark* is the protection of a distinctive name, word, phrase, symbol, or sign that distinguishes the goods or services of one manufacturer from those of others. Product names are trademarked.

Many people confuse the terms **trade name** and **trademark**. A trade name is a business name, whereas a particular product it sells is a trademark. For example, Levi Strauss is a trade name, and Dockers is a trademark. A **service mark** is like a trademark, but it refers to a service rather than a product.

The most common property for a small business to trademark is its identity, in the form of its logo, its product or service names, and its Internet domain name. In some cases, the overall appearance or look and feel of your stationery, your advertisements, your brochures, and/or your Web site can be protected through a type of trademark protection called *trade dress*. A trademark gives you the right to exclude other competitors from using names, symbols, or slogans that customers identify with your company.

The U.S. Copyright Office permits copyright registration of both graphical and textual elements. These elements might include drawings, photos, and product and company descriptions.

If you pay a consultant to create advertising or marketing materials, make sure that the copyright resides with you and not with that person. If possible, have the developer sign an agreement stating that you retain the copyright to whatever work is created.

# Checking Existing Records

Before you file to protect your property, you need to determine whether it is truly unique. The U.S. Patent and Trademark Office (PTO) has a searchable database that will tell you if your intellectual property has already been invented and protected. You can search for all three types of property protection online:

- **Patents.** http://www.uspto.gov/patft/index.html
- **Trademarks.** http://tess.uspto.gov
- **Copyrights.** http://www.loc.gov/copyright/rb.html

# Securing Your Patent, Trademark, or Copyright

The government agencies controlling patents, trademarks, and copyrights provide online forms that you can view, download, and print, so you can file your own application if you like. There is a nominal fee associated with applying (around $20). However, most people prefer to hire an attorney who specializes in intellectual property because the process can be complex.

You can also secure some rights simply by alerting people of your copyright to some material. For trademarks, you can place a ™ next to the item. If you have registered the trademark, you can use the ® symbol instead. You should also place a copyright notice on all your printed materials, such as brochures and Web sites. Include the word *copyright* along with the copyright symbol ©, your company's name, and the year that the work was published.

There's more to know about intellectual property law than I can possibly cover here. For more information, check out *Patent, Copyright & Trademark: A Desk Reference to Intellectual Property Law* by Stephen Elias or search the Web for "trademark law" or "intellectual property."

# Tax Planning

Many freelancers and home workers are very intimidated by tax filing, but there's no reason to be. It's not that much more difficult than filing taxes as someone else's employee.

 **NOTE** Remember, I'm not an accountant, and the information provided herein is not a substitute for legal or accounting advice from a professional. Research it yourself or hire a professional—either way, you need to become confident with your own tax situation rather than simply relying on the general advice here.

As a sole proprietor, you'll include your business on your own personal 1040 tax return, using a form called *Schedule C, Profit or Loss from Business*. If you have formed a corporation, the corporation must file a separate tax return. The information about tax filing in this book is focused primarily on the sole proprietorship because, if you have a corporation, you'll probably want to hire an accountant rather than doing your taxes on your own. (I'll cover incorporation later in this chapter, in case you're interested in pursuing that.)

The two big tax differences between you, a self-employed person, and someone who works for a company are

- ✪ You don't have an employer to withhold taxes from each paycheck, so you'll need to make quarterly estimated payments for state and federal taxes.

- ✪ You'll need to save the receipts for all your business expenses. If you plan to claim your home office as a deduction, you'll also need receipts for all your home expenses (electric bills, mortgage interest statements, and so on).

Most sole proprietors can do their own taxes using a program such as TurboTax for Business. Such programs walk you through your return preparation step by step, asking you questions and prompting you to enter amounts. In my experience, TurboTax does a good job, and it suggests many deductions that you might not have thought of.

I do my own taxes with TurboTax, but many of my freelancer friends swear by their accountants and maintain that their accountants find deductions that TurboTax would not have found for them. They claim that the tax savings more than pay for the accountant fees. Personally I'm skeptical of that claim, but I'll leave it up to you.

The IRS's Web site has a very helpful publication called *Starting a Business and Keeping Records* at http://www.irs.gov/forms_pubs/pubs/p583toc.htm. Look for publication 583.

**NOTE** Throughout this section of the book, I'll be referring you to various tax forms and publications. You can get them online from the IRS Web site at http://www.irs.gov/.

## Quarterly Tax Filing

As a self-employed person, tax time comes not once a year, but four times a year: April 15, June 15, September 15, and January 15. Your quarterly estimated tax payments are due on those dates. You'll fill out form 1040-ES and mail it in with your payment if you're a sole proprietor, or Form 1120-W for a corporation.

**TIP** If you expect to owe less than $1,000 in federal taxes in total for the tax year, including all your sources of income and all the withholding from any other employers, you do not have to file estimated taxes.

How much do you pay? That depends on how much you earned in the previous quarter and how much you expect to earn for the remainder of the tax year. See Publication 505 for instructions on estimating. I normally take the total amount of tax I paid for the previous year, add 10% to it, and divide it by four, and that's the payment I make. But if you use an accountant, he or she probably has a more sophisticated and accurate way of figuring it out.

● ● ● ● ● ● ● ● ● ● ● ● ● ● ● ● ● ● ● ● ● ● ● ● ● ● ● ● ● ● ● ● ● ● ● ● ● ● ● ● ● ● ● ●

Notice that the dates for quarterly filing are **not** exactly every three months; there are only 60 days between the first and second ones, and there are 120 days between the third and fourth.

● ● ● ● ● ● ● ● ● ● ● ● ● ● ● ● ● ● ● ● ● ● ● ● ● ● ● ● ● ● ● ● ● ● ● ● ● ● ● ● ● ● ● ●

There are several ways to pay your estimated tax. The traditional way is to mail your payment along with a Form 1040-ES. You can download 1040-ES from the IRS Web site the first time you file; after you file an estimated payment once, you will receive additional forms in the mail with already addressed envelopes for your future payments.

If you are getting a refund on your previous year's tax, you can apply that refund toward your future estimated payment. For example, suppose your tax return for the end of the year 2000 shows you getting a refund of $500. That return is due April 15, 2001. You figure that you will owe $2,000 for your first estimated payment in 2001, which is also due April 15, 2001. Simply enter the amount on line 67 of form 1040 (or line 42 of 1040A).

You can pay using electronic debit from a bank account rather than by writing a check, using the Electronic Federal Tax Payment System. For information about that, call 800-945-8400.

And finally, you can pay by credit card. (This comes in handy if you don't remember to pay until the day it's due!) To do so, call 888-272-9829. You can use Discover, American Express, MasterCard, or Visa. You will be charged a fee for the processing; this money goes to the company that handles the credit-card service, not to the IRS, depending on the amount. It's $3 for up to $99 payment, but the fee mounts up quickly if you make a large payment. For example, paying a quarterly tax bill of $5,000 would cost you $133 in fees. You can look up the exact amount of the fee online at http://www.8882paytax.com.

## Client Tax Requirements

If you do a lot of work for a particular client, the client might ask for your business ID number for tax-reporting purposes. That's your Social Security number if you're a sole proprietor. There's nothing fishy about them wanting that number—they're merely following the rules. The IRS requires companies to send a 1099-MISC form to each contractor to whom they pay more than $700 a year, and they need your ID number to file that form. Sometime between January 1 and February 28, you'll receive a 1099-MISC form from the client's accounting department, reporting how much money they paid you during the previous tax year.

Some clients might also ask you to fill out a W-4 form for tax withholding. It's merely a formality; fill it out with your SSN, your name, and your contact information, and indicate that you do not want them to withhold anything for taxes from your payment.

## Employees versus Independent Contractors

When you do work for a customer, you are an independent contractor, rather than an employee, right? Well, it depends. And it's important that you figure it out because of the tax consequences.

Generally speaking, the IRS uses the common law "right of control" test to determine worker status. Under this test, workers are employees if the people they work for have the right to direct and control the way they work—including the final results and the details of when, where, and how the job is accomplished. For example, if you go to an office every day, and work for specified hours, and are told what tools to use and in what order to accomplish the steps, you're an employee.

In contrast, the firms that hire them do not control independent contractors. A hiring firm's control is limited to accepting or rejecting the final results that an independent contractor achieves. So if you sit in your home office all day playing computer games and then do your work for the client from midnight to 6 a.m., and you can use whatever tools you want as long as the job gets done, you are an independent contractor.

What about telecommuters? They're classified as employees, because even though they work from home, the employer retains control over their hours and methods.

If you are considered an employee, the employer is legally required to take certain tax actions, such as withholding tax from your paycheck and making quarterly payments of it to the IRS and paying one half of your Social Security tax on that income. On the other hand, if you are considered an independent contractor, the customer pays you a certain amount flat out, and you are responsible for paying the taxes on that amount yourself.

Naturally, your customer will not want to consider you an employee because it will cost them time and money. So some companies have tried to wriggle out of the responsibility by claiming that some workers are independent contractors who are actually employees. Fortunately, if the IRS decides that you should have been hired as an employee rather than in independent contractor, the penalties and back taxes fall upon the employer, and not you as the employee.

# Record Keeping for Tax Deductions

To figure your taxes accurately at the end of the year, you will need good records of your income and expenses.

Using a good accounting software package like QuickBooks or Peachtree Complete is a great start. You must accurately record each transaction as it happens and not let yourself fall behind in this important duty. Whether you do your taxes yourself or hire an accountant, up-to-date business records are a must.

But when it comes to expenses, accounting records alone are not enough. In the event of an IRS audit, how will you prove that you actually spent $500 for a printer on March 12th? How will you prove that you paid $75 to have your office sprayed for ants on April 5th?

To have that proof, you'll need to save the receipts for everything you purchase for the business. I have a big envelope on my desk into which I stuff all the receipts for business expenses each week. Then at the end of the week, I sort and categorize them and enter them into my accounting program.

If you plan to deduct your home office on your taxes, you will also need to save all your utility bills and mortgage or rent payment stubs (if available). And if you have any work done on your house, such as roof repairs, save the receipts for those things too because you can deduct a portion of the cost as an indirect business expense. (More on this shortly.)

# Deducting Home Office Expenses

One of the advantages of working from home is that you're probably eligible for a tax deduction of your rent or mortgage, utilities, and other expenses as a business expense.

The basic rule for deducting a home office is that you must have a space that is used regularly and exclusively for your work. A home office does not need to be a separate room, but must be a clearly definable space. In addition to being regularly and exclusively used, this space must be one of the following:

- The primary place of work for this business (regular and exclusive use)
- A place where you meet with clients or customers
- A separate structure not connected to the house
- The sole place business inventory or product samples are stored

If none of the above is true, you don't qualify for the home-office deduction. Let's look at each of these qualifications in a bit more detail.

The first requirement for taking deductions related to your home is that you regularly use part of your home exclusively for a trade or business.

The notion of *regular use* is a bit vague. The IRS says it means you're using a part of your home for business on a continuing basis—not just for occasional or incidental business. A few hours a day on most days is probably enough to meet this test.

*Exclusive use* means that you use a portion of your home only for business. If you use part of your home for your business and also use it for personal purposes, you don't meet the exclusive use test. Remember in the Saturday morning session, I encouraged you to set aside a certain room or a certain area for business use only; that's because if you don't, you won't be able to pass the exclusive use test for the deduction.

Your home must be your "principal place of business"—or, alternatively, if your home isn't your principal place of business, you can qualify for the deduction if you meet clients or customers at home or if you use a separate structure on your property exclusively for business purposes.

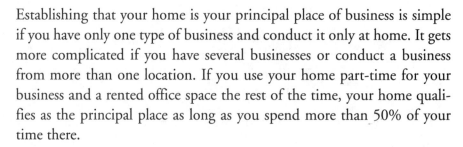

Establishing that your home is your principal place of business is simple if you have only one type of business and conduct it only at home. It gets more complicated if you have several businesses or conduct a business from more than one location. If you use your home part-time for your business and a rented office space the rest of the time, your home qualifies as the principal place as long as you spend more than 50% of your time there.

Your home doesn't have to be the place where you generate most of your business income. It's enough that you regularly use it to do such things as keeping your books, scheduling appointments, doing research, and ordering supplies. As long as you have no other fixed location where you do such things—for example, an outside office—you can take the deduction. For example, suppose you are a locksmith. You do most of your work out of your van, which contains all your tools. But you do your paperwork each night at your desk in your home office. The home office is deductible because your van is not a fixed location.

If your home isn't your principal place of business, you might still be entitled to deduct expenses for business use of your home if you regularly use part of your home exclusively to meet with clients, customers, or patients. Doing so even one or two days a week is probably sufficient.

**TIP**     Keep a log of the clients or customers you meet at home. Good records can be key if the IRS challenges your right to deduct home-related business expenses. Maintain an appointment book in which you carefully note the name of the client or customer and the date and time of each meeting at your home. Save these books for at least three years.

If your home isn't your principal place of business, and you don't meet clients or customers at home, you can deduct expenses for a separate, freestanding structure that you use regularly and exclusively for your

business. This might be a studio or a converted garage or barn, for example. The structure doesn't have to be your principal place of business or a place where you meet patients, clients, or customers. But be sure you use the structure only for your business: you can't store garden supplies there or, at least in theory, even use it for the monthly meeting of your investment club.

If you sell retail or wholesale products and you store inventory or samples at home, you can deduct expenses for the business use of your home. There are two limitations, however:

- You won't qualify for the deduction if you have an office or other business location away from your home.

- You have to store the products in a particular place—your garage, for example, or a closet or bedroom.

It's OK to use the storage space for other purposes as well, as long as you regularly use it for inventory or samples.

## Establishing Your Right to Claim a Home-Office Deduction

Here are some ways you can help establish the legal status of your home office:

- Take photos or make up a diagram showing the location of the office in your home, and include it in your business plan.

- Have business mail delivered to your home rather than to a post office box.

- Put your home address on your business cards and stationery.

- Have clients come to your home, and record their coming in your daily planner, so you can refer to it in the event of an audit.

- Store your inventory or samples in your home office.

## Why Deduct Home-Office Expenses?

There are three main benefits to the home-office deduction. First, when you deduct those otherwise personal expenses as business expenses, they not only reduce your income tax but also your self-employment tax.

Second, by claiming a home office, you're able to deduct rent, utilities, insurance, and depreciation that you can't otherwise take as expenses.

Finally, having a home office allows you to deduct more car expenses if you travel to do your work (for example, if you go to your clients' offices or homes as part of the job). Without a deductible office in your home, you generally cannot claim the miles you drive from home to your first business stop of the day and from your last stop of the day back home. This is considered non-deductible commuting mileage.

## Or Perhaps Not...

Some people decline to take the home-office deduction, even if they are eligible for it. Why? Because they think it will save them money in the long run. The home-office deduction includes depreciation of the portion of your home used for business. You get a small deduction each year for the depreciation, or "wear and tear," on your home.

If you later sell the property, you must pay tax on the depreciated portion as a business gain. Depending on many factors, including the selling price of your home, the portion of it you use for the office, and the number of years you have used it for business, you might find that the money you save little by little over the years of deducting your home office is not worth the big hit later when you sell. It's a little more complex than that, so you might want to consult an accountant or financial planner if you are unsure whether deducting your home office is right for you.

 **NOTE** Keep in mind that whether or not you can deduct expenses that relate specifically to your home, such as rent, utilities, home insurance, and repairs, you can still take a deduction for regular business expenses, such as photocopies, stationery, paper clips, wages, travel, equipment, professional memberships, and publications. You can also deduct the cost of long-distance calls you make from home and a separate phone line used for business calls.

## Direct versus Indirect Expenses

If you decide to take a home-office deduction, and you are entitled to do so, you will need to meticulously save every receipt from every expense for your home. This can include an expense for the home in general as well as an expense specific to your office space. Then, at tax time, you'll divide the receipts into two piles:

- ✿ **Direct.** A *direct expense* is an expense related only to the home-office portion of the home. For example, if you paid an electrician to run a separate electrical line to your office, that's a direct expense. The cost of a baseboard heater installed in your attic so that your office there will be warm enough for winter work would also be a direct expense. You get the idea.

- ✿ **Indirect.** An indirect expense is an expense for the home or property as a whole. For example, if you pay a monthly fee for pest control for your home, that's indirect. They spray the office, but they also spray the rest of the house. Your utility bills are also indirect expenses.

 **NOTE** If you use a tax-preparation program such as TurboTax, it will figure out your percentages and place the numbers on the correct forms automatically. I can't imagine doing my own taxes without one of these programs!

When organizing your indirect expenses, don't forget these:

- **Mortgage interest and real estate taxes**. Your mortgage interest and real estate taxes are indirect expenses. You can then deduct the remainder of the amounts (the non-business portions) on your *Schedule A, Itemized Deductions*.

- **Cleaning**. If you have a housekeeper or cleaning service that cleans your home, you can deduct that as an indirect expense for your home office (assuming they clean your office room as part of the service).

- **Lawn care**. If you use a lawn-care service for your home, that bill can be deducted as an indirect home office expense too.

- **Home repairs and improvements**. If you improve or repair your home, such as replacing your old air conditioner or having a new sidewalk poured, you can deduct it as an indirect expense.

## Calculating Your Deduction

To calculate your home-office deduction, you'll use Form 8829, *Expenses for Business Use of Your Home*. It walks you through the various deductions step by step, allowing you to enter direct and indirect expenses in a variety of categories.

Form 8829 (lines 1 through 7) helps you figure what percentage of your home is used for your home office. There are two ways to calculate this. You can take the square footage of the office and divide it by the total square footage of your home; alternatively, if the rooms are all about the same size, you can take a fraction based on the number of rooms used for business versus the total number of rooms. For example, there are six rooms in my house, and I use one for business, so my business percentage of the home is $\frac{1}{6}$, or 16.67%.

**TIP** If you have a separate bathroom that you use only when you are in your office, and nobody else ever uses it for personal use, you could deduct it as a room in your office too.

Then as you work through the form, you multiply the total of your indirect expenses by the business-use percentage you calculated, and then add that amount to 100% of your direct expenses. That gives you your allowable expenses (line 34).

The form also calculates your depreciation on your home for business use. This can be a little tricky, because you need to know your home's adjusted basis and its fair market value, and be able to state the smaller of the two. You'll also need to know the value of the land on which the home is built. See the instructions for the form (available at http://www.irs.gov) for help, or talk to an accountant.

## Often-Overlooked Business Deductions

Besides your home office expenses, there are tons of deductions you can take as a business owner. Here are some ideas to get you thinking.

**CAUTION** Again, remember that I'm not an accountant and this is not professional advice I'm giving you here. Your situation might be such that some of these deductions aren't allowable. See an accountant or contact the IRS if you're not sure.

○ **Subscriptions**. Do you subscribe to any publications or newspapers related to your profession? They might be deductible. For example, as a computer technician, I might deduct my *PC Magazine* subscription.

- **Books**. If you buy books related to your profession for your professional library, you might be able to deduct them. For example, a computer technician might deduct the purchase of a book on computer upgrading and repair.

- **Online services**. If you use your Internet ISP or Web-hosting service exclusively for business, you can deduct it. You can't deduct it, however, if you also use it for personal things or if you share it with family members.

- **Car and truck expenses**. If you used a vehicle for business, you can deduct the mileage for it, or a portion of its actual expenses, using form 4562, *Depreciation and Amortization*. Enter car and truck expenses in Part V.

- **Casualties and thefts**. If any of your business property was lost, stolen, or damaged, you can deduct it. For example, last year my purse was stolen, and it contained my Palm III with all my business contacts in it. I was able to deduct its replacement value on form 4684, *Casualties and Thefts*. I didn't claim my purse's cost because it was not exclusively for business use, but if it had been my briefcase, I could have claimed its replacement value too.

## Depreciating Capital Equipment

When you buy big-ticket items for your business (such as a backhoe for a construction company or a panel truck for a moving company), you must depreciate it—spread out its cost over its useful life. (There's an exception to this rule, though, which I'll explain shortly.)

For example, suppose you bought a humidifier for your office for $500. You expect it to last five years. You don't deduct the full $500 on your taxes in the year you make the purchase; you spread out the expense over your taxes for the next five years, using the formulas provided on Form 4562, *Depreciation and Amortization*. This form offers many different

kinds of depreciation, ranging from three-year property to 25-year property, as well as special sections for residential and non-residential real estate.

Depreciation can be a real pain to calculate, and if you need to buy a lot of equipment for your business start up, it can really hurt your company's bottom line initially, because you are paying taxes on money that you have already spent for the business on legitimate expenses. So fortunately, the IRS offers an allowance called Section 179. You can deduct up to a certain amount (in 1999 it was $19,000) of certain types of purchases fully on your taxes for the year in which you made the purchase, without having to depreciate.

You can enter the purchases that you wish to claim a Section 179 exemption for on line 6 of Form 4562, *Depreciation and Amortization.* There is room for only one item on the form, but you can attach an *Additional Section 179 Property Statement* to list any other items. I deduct all my computer equipment purchases this way because I'm never quite sure how long these items will last before they break or become obsolete.

◆ ◆ ◆ ◆ ◆ ◆ ◆ ◆ ◆ ◆ ◆ ◆ ◆ ◆ ◆ ◆ ◆ ◆ ◆ ◆ ◆ ◆ ◆ ◆ ◆ ◆ ◆ ◆ ◆ ◆ ◆ ◆ ◆ ◆ ◆ ◆ ◆ ◆ ◆ ◆ ◆

Depreciation can sometimes be good. For example, suppose you buy a big-ticket item for the business and make monthly payments on it. If you took the entire cost as a Section 179 deduction the first year, your business would not be able to deduct the payments in future years, nor any of the interest paid on the loan. Check with an accountant if you are not sure of the most advantageous way to deduct a particular item.

◆ ◆ ◆ ◆ ◆ ◆ ◆ ◆ ◆ ◆ ◆ ◆ ◆ ◆ ◆ ◆ ◆ ◆ ◆ ◆ ◆ ◆ ◆ ◆ ◆ ◆ ◆ ◆ ◆ ◆ ◆ ◆ ◆ ◆ ◆ ◆ ◆ ◆ ◆ ◆ ◆

Again, let me encourage you to use a tax-preparation software program if you plan to figure your own taxes. A good program will help you determine which expenses are eligible for Section 179 and which are not. Software, for example, is not eligible. Don't try to wing it on your own with an ink pen and a stack of paper forms, because the rules are rather complex and you're sure to get some of it wrong.

# Should You Incorporate?

When I first started my business, I wondered whether I should incorporate, although I wasn't sure why it was a good thing. And the more people I talked to, the more confused about it I became. It seemed that everyone had a strong opinion, and everyone's opinion was different.

Your home business is probably a sole proprietorship—that is, it has only one owner, and that's you. Being a sole proprietorship business is administratively easy, which is especially good for those of us who are not interested in meticulous accounting and record keeping. As a sole proprietor, you file your business taxes and your personal taxes together under your Social Security number. All business profits are assumed to be your personal profits, and all business losses are your personal losses.

In contrast, when you incorporate your business, the paperwork increases exponentially. Incorporation itself involves paperwork and fees. You must establish a board of directors, who must hold regular meetings in which you take formal minutes and keep them on file. You will definitely need a professional accountant if you don't have one already. You'll need a business ID number that's different from your Social Security number, and the corporation will file its own tax return separate from your own.

So why would people voluntarily put themselves through all that administrative headache? Well, being incorporated does have some advantages. Are the advantages enough to justify the hassle? That's up to you to decide.

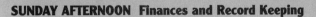

Here are some of the advantages of a corporation:

- **Income belongs to the corporation, not the individual.** The corporation pays you a salary. As a personal taxpayer, you are responsible for paying tax only on that salary. The corporation, however, pays tax on the rest of the profit, so you're not really saving much. The primary benefit is to pay yourself a low salary that puts you in a lower tax bracket than you would otherwise be in.

- **Corporations can offer more tax-flexible pension plans and greater medical deductions than sole proprietorships.** This is not a big issue unless you have multiple employees, though, and most home businesses do not. Besides, few start-up companies have the cash flow needed to take full advantage.

- **A corporation can shield you from liability from business debts and lawsuits.** If the corporation goes bankrupt, you as an individual do not. And if an unhappy customer sues the corporation, your personal assets cannot be seized.

- **A corporation is a more attractive borrower to a bank than a sole proprietor.** That means you might be able to get better business loans.

You have three basic business structures from which to choose:

- Sole proprietorship
- Partnership (limited or general)
- Corporation (S, C or LLC)

I've already talked in some detail about sole proprietorships, so now look at the other options.

**NOTE** The legal structure you choose depends on a number of things, including your type of business, your individual situation, goals for the business, and a number of other personal and financial factors. Before deciding what's best for you, discuss your plans with your accountant and attorney. Make sure you are prepared to describe your business plans in some detail. It will be money and time well spent. Making the right choice can help you avoid a mistake that can cost you a lot in terms of possible future liability.

## Partnerships

This type of business is just what the name implies: Business ownership is divided between two or more partners. The *general partnership* is the most common and is formed to conduct a business with two or more partners being fully involved in the operation of the business. All the partners share both profits and liabilities.

A *limited partnership*, as the name implies, provides for limited liability of the partners. This liability can be no greater than the partner's investment in the partnership. In a limited partnership, there must be a least one general partner who remains liable for all the debts of the partnership. Forming a partnership is complex and legal advice is very important. The kind of partnership and the type of partner you will be determines your potential personal liability.

The advantages of a partnership include the following:

- ✪ The partnership itself does not pay federal income taxes. An informational tax return (Form 1065) must be filed for the partnership, showing the pass-through of all the profit and loss to each partner.
- ✪ Liability can be spread among the partners.
- ✪ Start-up money can come from the partners in the form of a loan to the partnership, which creates interest income for the partners and a business deduction for the partnership.

The disadvantages are as follows:

- Forming a partnership and making changes to one are complex legal matters requiring an attorney.
- Problems between the partners (misunderstandings, conflicts, and so on) can cause problems for the business.
- Limited partners are liable for debt if they are active managers in the business. General partners have unlimited liability. You might also be liable for the commitments made by a partner.

# Corporations

You establish a corporation in a certain state, and you are allowed to conduct business only in that state. Of course, you can do business with customers in other states, but your main headquarters must be in the state in which you incorporate.

It is essential to obtain legal advice if you are thinking about forming a corporation. Because each state has its own set of corporation laws, you should contact the appropriate office in your state (usually the office of the Secretary of State) for additional material and procedures. Most offices can provide a guide for new businesses to follow for incorporation and doing business in their state. Call or write for a copy.

The most common reason for forming a corporation is to minimize personal liability, but a corporation might not always provide a perfect liability shield. The liability of stockholders (owners) in a corporation is limited under certain and complex conditions. However, there is no such thing as total insulation from liability resulting from doing business as a corporation.

Record keeping and tax matters with a corporation are difficult and time-consuming tasks, usually requiring the services of an accountant. You need to keep this in mind when considering operating costs for your business.

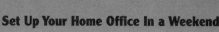

Avoid the "do it yourself" incorporation guides. Incorporating is a complex process, and you should not take on the task yourself. You cannot afford any mistakes at this point in your new business, so if you decide incorporation is for you, do it right and spend the money required to have it done professionally. Legal fees for setting up a corporation can run between $350 and $1,500 (assuming the corporation is relatively straightforward).

There are three major types of corporations:

♦ The C-corporation ("regular corporation")

♦ The S-corporation (or "S-Corp")

♦ The Limited Liability Corporation (or "LLC")

I'll explain the differences below.

## Regular Corporations

A regular corporation is the type of corporation most people think of when they hear the word *incorporated*. The corporation is a legal, taxable entity with a board of directors.

The advantages of a regular corporation are as follows:

♦ Shareholders (the owners) have personal limited liability for business debts and lawsuits.

♦ It is usually easier to obtain business capital for a regular corporation than with other legal structures.

♦ Profits can be divided among owners and the corporation in order to reduce taxes by taking advantage of lower tax rates.

♦ The corporation does not dissolve upon the death of a stockholder (owner) or if ownership changes.

- The corporation gets favorable tax deductions for providing employee fringe benefits including medical-, disability-, and life-insurance plans.

- If the corporation owns stock investments, 70% of any dividends it receives from those investments are deductible (unless the corporation purchased the stock with borrowed money).

The disadvantages of a regular corporation are as follows:

- It's more expensive and complex to set up than other legal structures.

- Completing tax returns usually requires the help of an accountant.

- There is double taxation on profits paid to owners. (The corporation pays corporate taxes on profits and the owner pays personal taxes on dividends from the corporation.)

- There are annual fees to pay to maintain the corporation.

- Tax rates are higher than individual rates for profits greater than approximately $75,000.

- There is a 28% accumulated earnings tax on profits in excess of $250,000.

- Business losses are not deductible by the corporation.

## S-Corporation

The S-corporation offers the limited-liability advantages of a corporation but does not pay federal taxes. All the earnings and losses of an S-corporation are passed through to the shareholders. It is a popular form of incorporation in the start-up years of a business because of the limited amount of extra paperwork. However, there are some subtle disadvantages that need to be taken into account as your business grows. Again, because of the complexities involved, talk with your attorney and accountant.

The advantages of an S-corporation are as follows:

- Owners enjoy limited personal liability as in a regular corporation.
- There is no federal income tax liability and, in most cases, no state income tax. The owners pay the taxes on their personal tax returns.
- Profit/losses are passed to owners directly, so there is no double taxation.
- The S-corporation does not dissolve if one of the owners dies or otherwise leaves (as in a regular corporation).
- Wholly owned subsidiaries are permitted.

The disadvantages of an S-corporation are as follows:

- You'll need legal assistance to set it up.
- A maximum of 75 shareholders is permitted
- Only one class of stock can be issued, so you cannot have common and preferred stock types.

## Limited Liability Corporation (LLC)

This type of corporation blends the tax advantages of a partnership and the limited-liability advantages of a corporation. As you might expect, it also has some limitations as your business grows, but is definitely worth considering. Ask about the LLC when you contact your appropriate state office for incorporation information.

The advantages of an LLC are as follows:

- Limited personal liability for the owners (like a corporation).
- No federal taxes (like a partnership).
- No limit on the number of stockholders (like a regular corporation).

- More than one class of stock is permitted (like a regular corporation).
- Business losses might be deducted on your personal tax return (like an S-corporation).

The disadvantages of an LLC are as follows:

- Legal assistance is required to set up the LLC, and the paperwork is somewhat complex.
- There is no "continuity of life" as in a regular corporation. The LLC dissolves if one of the owners dies or otherwise leaves. However, other formal agreements between the owners can overcome this.
- Some states require that an LLC have more than one member, so you might not be able to set one up without at least one business partner.

## Forming Your Corporation

If you decide that some sort of corporation is your best bet, your first step should be to hire a competent accountant and/or attorney to help you through the process. Then, guided by the professional you choose, you will complete the following steps:

1. **Choose the state in which you will incorporate.** In most cases, this should be the state in which you operate your business. That's the least complicated and most cost-effective way. However, some business owners prefer the advantages of forming a corporation in a specific state, such as Delaware or Nevada, with favorable incorporation regulations.

2. **Choose a name for your corporation.** It must not be the same as that of any other incorporated business in the state in which you incorporate. Do a trademark search as described earlier in the chapter to make sure your name is unique.

3.  **Choose the corporation type (regular, S-corporation, or LLC).**

4.  **Decide whether you will have a general business corporation, a close corporation, a professional corporation, or a not-for-profit corporation.** Your lawyer or accountant will explain the differences and consequences of this choice.

5.  **Decide what classes of stock you will issue.** There are two basic kinds: common and preferred. Common stockholders have voting rights; preferred stockholders do not. However, preferred stock gets preferential treatment in dividend distribution.

6.  **Get a corporate kit.** These are generally available at office-supply stores and include a corporate seal, stock certificates, a stock ledger, and sample minutes and bylaws.

7.  **Decide on your board of directors.** These are people who will manage the company and establish the policies (the bylaws). They also elect corporate officers, usually during the organizational meeting. Different states have varying requirements as to the number of directors requires.

8.  **Determine the corporate address.** Most states require you to have a corporate address at the time of incorporation. For a home-based business, this will probably be your home address.

9.  **Choose a registered agent.** State law requires that a person or entity located within the state of incorporation be available during business hours to receive legal notices. If you are not physically located in the state, you will need to hire someone to fill this function. Most people use a lawyer for the registered agent.

## Holding Corporate Meetings

After the initial filing, corporations are required to follow certain formalities in order to maintain their corporate status. These formalities vary from state to state, and include a variety of shareholder and director meetings.

It's very important to hold these meetings according to the regulations of your state. If a corporation fails to follow corporate formalities and you run into legal or financial trouble, the corporate entity can potentially be disregarded and the owners held personally liable for corporation debts.

The following documents should be maintained with the corporate records:

- Minutes of the original organizing meeting for the corporation
- Minutes of the annual directors' meeting
- Minutes from the annual shareholder meeting
- Minutes from any special meetings held throughout the year
- Copies of any bylaws or resolutions that were approved during any meetings

Meeting minutes do not need to be filed with the state. Purchasing a corporate kit will make complying with these formalities an easy task. A good kit will provide the necessary sample forms and instructions on how to conduct the meetings properly.

## Corporate Bylaws

Your bylaws govern the internal affairs of the corporation and define the rights and obligations of the corporation's officers, directors, and shareholders. You don't need to file these with the state; they are for internal corporate use only. They state specific rules regarding corporate governance, including the procedures for holding director and shareholder meetings, the number of directors of the corporation, and what officer positions the corporation will have (president, vice-president, secretary, treasurer, and so on).

Because this document controls the internal governance of the corporation, it should be referred to whenever the corporation needs to take action on any matter. This is very important! For example, if the bylaws

state that the board of directors will meet annually in June, you can't have the annual meeting in July or August instead without making a formal change through proper procedure (usually a vote of the board).

The directors typically write the bylaws at their initial organizing meeting. Many of these are boilerplate and can be taken from a kit, but you should review any prewritten bylaws carefully before adopting them to make sure they make sense for your company. Make the bylaws adoption part of the formal minutes of the initial meeting.

If the needs of the corporation change, the bylaws can be easily amended. No state filing is required; a simple affirmative vote of the directors or shareholders will suffice.

# Do You Take Credit Cards?

Being able to take credit cards can be a huge boon to a small business, especially one that does a lot of selling over the phone or the Internet. Traditionally, however, it has been difficult for home office users to find a bank that will let them open a merchant account to do so.

These days, there are two kinds of providers of credit card services: banks and independent services organizations (ISOs). Banks offer greater security and stability but are picky about their clients and charge higher fees. ISOs are more tolerant of high-risk accounts, such as start-up companies, but they are not monitored and regulated to the same extent as banks and might be less dependable.

◆ ◆ ◆ ◆ ◆ ◆ ◆ ◆ ◆ ◆ ◆ ◆ ◆ ◆ ◆ ◆ ◆ ◆ ◆ ◆ ◆ ◆ ◆ ◆ ◆ ◆ ◆ ◆ ◆ ◆ ◆ ◆ ◆ ◆ ◆ ◆ ◆ ◆ ◆ ◆

**CAUTION**    Be especially cautious about ISOs that do not require you to open a merchant account. Many of these services offer to process your orders through a merchant account in their name, not yours. It might be difficult to gain access to your money if there are any disputes between you and the ISO.

◆ ◆ ◆ ◆ ◆ ◆ ◆ ◆ ◆ ◆ ◆ ◆ ◆ ◆ ◆ ◆ ◆ ◆ ◆ ◆ ◆ ◆ ◆ ◆ ◆ ◆ ◆ ◆ ◆ ◆ ◆ ◆ ◆ ◆ ◆ ◆ ◆ ◆ ◆ ◆

First, you'll need to find a provider. Try going to your own bank and asking if it can offer this service to you. Be careful, however, because many banks deal with agents who in turn represent an electronic clearinghouse. These agents are commissioned and are not looking out for your interests.

If your bank won't help (and it probably won't), you can find many providers by searching the Internet. Most listings will be agents who represent an electronic clearinghouse or the clearinghouse houses themselves. Remember, talk only to the clearinghouses directly.

Next, compare the costs for the services that you find available. Your merchant status will require that you pay a discount rate on each transaction. These rates are always higher for businesses that don't have a brick-and-mortar store front; however, you should not pay much over 2%. A transaction fee is also charged, which should be around 20–30¢. Don't pay more.

If you'll process customer credit cards physically at your office, you will need a terminal (or software) to enter credit-card data and to obtain authorization for the charge. This is where many providers make the bulk of their money. Terminal costs range from $200 to $2,000 (and they are all basically the same).

If you plan to process credit cards by phone or Internet, you'll want software instead of a terminal. There are two major software products for this purpose: IC Verify and PC Authorize (each around $350). Overall, the software is a much better deal if you have a PC and won't be doing a lot of business in person. IC Verify is a much more full-featured program, but a home worker is unlikely to need all those features, such as the capability to hook up a terminal to the PC and switch between software-entered transactions and swiped ones.

When selecting a provider, watch out for fees. Here are the legitimate fees that most providers will charge:

- ✪ **Statement fee.** The fee for receiving a paper statement of your activity. Probably about $10 a month.
- ✪ **Transaction fee.** Around 20–30¢ per transaction.

Some ISOs try to stick you for other fees, such as application fees, setup fees, minimum account billing, chargebacks, voice authorization, and daily close-out, but these are all rip offs. Find a provider that doesn't charge them.

Some other things to look for in a provider include customer support, a toll-free number, a warranty on equipment, and a free manual imprinter. You should also ask when your funds will be available (should be no more than three days) and what credit cards can be taken (Visa and Mastercard at the minimum).

**TIP** If all this seems like way too much trouble for the few credit-card transactions you think you'll need to accept, consider a free Internet service such as PayPal (http://www.pay-pal.com). A favorite service of Internet auction folk on Ebay (http://www.ebay.com), PayPal allows individuals to send and receive money on their credit cards through a secure server. Confirmations are handled through e-mail.

# Getting Affordable Insurance

When people first make the leap from employee to self-employed, they worry a lot about insurance. I've even heard people say "I would love to work for myself, but I need my insurance."

Most of these people don't realize that there are other ways of getting insurance than as a benefit from an employer, and it doesn't have to be all

that expensive. My health insurance is equivalent to what I received from my last employer, for example, and it costs me less than $100 a month. Because I make at least $100 a month more on my own than I did at my last job (and then some!), the cost is more than covered.

In the following sections, I'll tell you a little about the various kinds of insurance you might want to have as a self-employed person.

## Homeowner or Renter Insurance

You probably already have homeowners insurance (or renters insurance if you rent rather than own your home). But most homeowner policies specifically exclude business use of your home, so if you have a loss related to your business, you're out of luck. The solution: Contact your insurance agent and purchase additional coverage to include your home business.

## Health Insurance

Under COBRA law, when you leave full-time employment that includes insurance benefits, you can purchase the same insurance benefits that you enjoyed as an employee for up to 18 months from the company that you left. This is useful if you have many medical problems and would have a hard time getting private insurance coverage, but it can be rather expensive. When I looked into it several years ago, it was going to cost over $300 a month for a healthy 30-year-old non-smoker, and that seemed high to me.

The good news is that there are lots of insurance companies that would like your health-insurance business, and many of them offer better deals than COBRA.

If you are a basically healthy person who sees a physician only infrequently, look into a high-deductible Major Medical plan. Such plans do not cover routine care, but in the event of an accident or serious disease, they will absorb most of the cost. These plans are fairly cheap, too. Rather than being "health plans" that pay your medical expenses in full, they're insurance in the true sense of the word—a shield against disaster.

You might be able to get health insurance through membership in an association such as NASE (National Association for the Self Employed). Their Web site, on which you can find more information, is http://www.nase.com. But don't assume that any group policy is necessarily a better deal than any individual policy. That's not the case at all.

I have shopped around for insurance quite a bit, and have found that the best deal for me is a high-deductible individual policy through Blue Cross/Blue Shield. Because it is a not-for-profit company, it can afford to offer rates that are more reasonable than those offered by some of the large insurance conglomerates that must make a profit to satisfy shareholders. You can check out Blue Cross/Blue Shield at http://www.blue-cares.com.

## Disability Insurance

What do you think your most valuable business asset is? Is it your computer? Your business vehicle? Your home office? Nope, none of those things. Your most valuable asset is your ability to work. Over your lifetime, you will make more money from this ability than from any other asset.

Disability insurance is protection of that asset. It protects your income if you are unable to work for an extended period of time. If you become disabled and are unable to make a living, disability insurance will pay you a salary.

Now the bad news: It is difficult for self-employed people to get disability insurance through traditional insurance companies, especially those who spend the majority of their workday in a home office. That's because disability is so hard to verify for such people that the insurance companies run a big risk of being ripped off. Many insurance companies won't even talk to a home worker looking for a disability policy.

Although I have not dealt with them personally, a fellow freelancer, Tim Huddleston, tells me that The Principal Financial Group is a good company for disability insurance. He says they understand self-employed people's needs better than the average company. You can check them out at http://www.principal.com. Tim also notes:

> Never, ever use the term *freelancer* to describe yourself to an insurance company. They'll slam the door immediately. You might as well call yourself an itinerant worker. Instead, describe yourself as a self-employed person or as a sole proprietor. They respect that. Be completely honest with the insurer and be prepared to provide complete tax returns and financial history for the past three years. If you tend to work without signed contracts, ask three of your best clients to write "To Whom It May Concern" letters verifying your status as a contractor. The letter does not need to promise future employment—only to verify that you have a track record as a contractor.

One more thing: If you get disability insurance, do not write off the premiums as a business expense. (In some states, you can't do this anyway.) If you write them off, the benefits will be taxed at your current tax rate. If you eat the expense, the benefits are tax-free.

Assuming you are able to find an insurer who will grant you disability insurance, what should you look for? The details of disability insurance can vary greatly between policies. Here are some of the variables.

## Waiting Period

Some policies kick in immediately when you become disabled; others don't start paying until you have been disabled for a certain amount of time, such as six months.

Policies that pay immediately are much more expensive than ones with a delay, so it is most cost-effective to get a policy with a rather long delay period and then simply sock away enough money in your savings account to support yourself for the number of months until the insurance starts paying.

## Chosen Profession

Some policies specify that you will be paid if you are unable to work in your "chosen profession," which means whatever you were doing for a living when the disability occurred. Other policies won't pay unless you are sufficiently disabled as to be unable to work in any job.

Even though they cost more, "chosen profession" policies are preferable. This is because if you can't do what you're best at, you might be stuck in some menial job that doesn't pay very well, and yet you wouldn't be receiving any insurance benefits.

## Duration of Benefits

Some policies will continue to pay for the rest of your working life (until retirement age) or until you become able to work, whichever comes first. Others have a fixed duration, such as five years.

I look at disability insurance the same way I do medical insurance—it's for catastrophic situations only. So I look for a disability policy with a long wait before benefits start and a long duration of payment. I figure I can survive if I'm laid up for six months or a year, but if I get knocked out of the workforce more-or-less permanently, I want to be taken care of until I'm ready to retire.

## Partial Benefits for Part-Time Work

Some disability policies offer partial benefits when you go back to work but are not healthy enough to work full-time. This is a plus because you can use it while you ease yourself back into the workforce.

## Guaranteed Renewability

A guaranteed-renewable, non-cancelable policy means the insurance company can't raise your premium or cancel your disability insurance as long as you pay your premiums.

## Inflation Protection

If you get insurance that pays for many years, such as up until you retire, make sure the policy includes inflation protection. That ensures that your disability benefits will be increased to keep pace with inflation after a disability begins.

## Guaranteed Future Insurability

This means you can increase your disability income insurance as your salary increases without proving medical assurability.

## Premium Waiver After Disability

This ensures that if you become disabled, your premiums would automatically be waived until you're no longer disabled. Believe it or not, some policies expect you to continue to make insurance payments while they're paying *you*!

## Return of Premium

This rider refunds a portion of the premiums you've paid if you stay healthy.

# Business Liability Insurance and Bonding

Business liability insurance pays off in the event that someone successfully sues you for shoddy workmanship or poor performance of your job. It's kind of like malpractice insurance for nondoctors.

Most businesses don't really need this kind of insurance unless they perform a service or provide a product that has expensive consequences if performed or made improperly. For example, a writer or editor would probably not need liability insurance, but a motorcycle repairperson or a lawyer might.

*Bonding* is akin to liability insurance, except it's for individuals rather than for the business as a whole. You pay a bonding company a fee, and it takes responsibility if a certain person does something wrong.

There are many different kinds of bonds; bail bonds are one type that everyone has heard of. Bail-bonding companies get a fee for posting bail for someone who has been arrested. If the person shows up for court, the bail-bonding company gets its money back; if not, it loses the money.

People who go into homes or businesses unsupervised are commonly bonded. If you have employees who represent you, bonding them protects you if the person steals or damages something or fails to perform his or her duties properly. Customers often prefer to work with bonded individuals because they feel more confident that the bonded individual is trustworthy.

# Your Retirement Plan

As a self-employed person, you don't have the advantage of an employer-sponsored retirement savings plan. That doesn't mean you'll be bereft when you retire, however; it simply means you must take charge of your retirement plan yourself.

Many people work with a financial planner to set up their retirement strategy, and that's a really good idea if you aren't sure what you want and don't know much about investing. But the important thing is to con-

tribute the maximum allowable amount to your retirement plan each year to maximize your tax benefits.

There are dozens of different types of retirement plans, but I'll focus here on three that are most useful for self-employed sole proprietors: IRA, SEP-IRA, and Roth IRA. Each of these retirement plans can be held at any of a variety of financial institutions, including banks, credit unions, and brokerages, and can be invested in individual stocks, money-market funds, mutual funds, or other investments.

- **Regular IRA.** Anyone can open an Individual Retirement Account (IRA) and contribute up to $2,000 a year to it. The money you contribute is tax-deductible, and the money grows in the IRA tax-free. You can begin withdrawing money from it when you reach retirement age. At that point, you pay taxes on the money as if it were regular income you were receiving from an employer. You must start making withdrawals when you reach age 70 1/2.

- **SEP-IRA.** This is an IRA for self-employed people and small businesses. As a sole proprietor, you can contribute up to 15% of your income to your SEP-IRA each year, which makes it much more advantageous than a regular IRA. If you have employees, the employees can contribute to their own SEP-IRA accounts and you as the employer can also contribute to their accounts for them. As with a regular IRA, deposits are tax-deductible, and the money grows tax-free until withdrawn. You must start making withdrawals at age 70 1/2.

- **Roth IRA.** When you make contributions to a Roth IRA, the contributions are not tax-deductible. However, when you reach retirement age, you can begin withdrawing from the Roth IRA tax-free. This can be a really good deal if you have many years left before retirement, because the money will grow over the years and you won't ever have to pay tax on the increase. You can convert an existing IRA to a Roth IRA, but you must pay tax on the money at the time of conversion. You do not have to start making withdrawals at any certain age.

To open an IRA, choose the financial institution you want to go through and fill out an application there. I won't attempt to advise you on choosing a financial institution or investing your money, but I will tell you this much: Don't be too conservative. The longer you have until retirement, the more aggressive you should be. Create a well-balanced portfolio that includes both risky and safe investments, but don't cheat yourself out of big profits over the long term by staying exclusively with conservative investments.

**TIP**

Some experts say that you should invest a percentage of your retirement money in conservative investments such as money-market funds, bonds, and certificates of deposit according to your age. A 35 year old person should have 35% invested conservatively, a 60 year old person 60%, and so on.

I have no special expertise as a financial planner, but I can tell you what has worked for me. My personal retirement portfolio consists of the following:

- A regular IRA that I created when I rolled over funds from my previous employer's retirement plan. I do not contribute to this account anymore, but it continues to grow tax-deferred.

- A SEP-IRA that I contribute to aggressively to the maximum extent possible (15% per year). I use TurboTax at the end of the year to compute my maximum payment, and then make a final lump-sum payment to my account to exactly match that maximum.

My regular IRA is invested in individual high-tech stock picks. Once a year or so I evaluate this portfolio of stocks and make buys and sells based on each company's performance. This account is held at a low-commission online brokerage that does not charge any yearly maintenance fees.

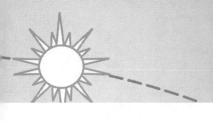
My SEP-IRA is invested in a variety of mutual funds with varying degrees of risk. About 50% of my SEP-IRA is in an aggressive, high-technology mutual fund that has wild ups and downs in the short term. But because I'm in it for the long term, I know that over the long haul, this fund will pay off better than the safer ones. An additional 20% is in a moderately aggressive international fund that invests in non-U.S. companies. The final 30% is in a relatively safe mutual fund of large, well-established U.S. companies.

# Congratulations!

You made it to the end of the weekend! I hope this has been a productive time for you, and that you're brimming with ideas and enthusiasm for setting up your office, starting your business, and planning for your future success.

If this book has been helpful to you, I would love to hear about it. Please drop me a line c/o Prima Publishing at the address found on the credits page at the beginning of the book, or e-mail me at faithe@wempen.com. Best wishes with your business!

APPENDIX A

# Home Office
# Online Resources

Here's a list of some of the most helpful Web sites for home office workers and small-/home-business owners.

# Accounting

### http://www.quickbooks.com

This is the home page of the QuickBooks program, providing program help, some general business accounting information, and referrals to certified accounting professionals in your area who can work with Quick-Books data.

### http://www.peachtree.com

This is the home page of Peachtree software, maker of the Peachtree Complete Accounting program. Program updates are available as well as a free trial version.

# Advice

### http://www.score.org

The Service Corps of Retired Executives offers answers to common business questions from experienced professionals.

### http://www.americanexpress.com/smallbusiness

At this Web site, you'll find lots of free advice on many aspects of running a business.

# Auctions

### http://www.ebay.com

This is the biggest and best place to buy and sell items. Buying is free; selling costs 1–5 percent of the sale price and a small listing fee.

### http://www.auctionwatch.com

This agent site lists all the auctions at multiple auction sites that match your entered criteria.

### http://www.auctionwatchers.com

This auction monitoring site that is very similar to the preceding one.

### http://www.onsale.com

Combined with http://www.Egghead.com, this site lists computer hardware and software, electronics, home gadgets, and even vacations for auction. You can only buy—not sell.

# Banking

### http://www.livecapital.com

Fill out a single form to apply for a business loan at over two dozen banks at once.

### http://www.paytrust.com

This site offers a Web-based bill-payment service, which costs about $9 a month.

## http://www.quicken.com/banking_and_credit

Part of the Quicken.com Web site, this area offers lots of good advice and information about banking, both online and in your local community.

# Business Plans

### http://www.sbaonline.sba.gov

The U.S. Small Business Administration offers a business plan tutorial with sample plans and local resource listings on this Web site.

### http://www.bplans.com

Acquire business plan samples and interactive tools from Palo Alto software at this Web site.

### http://www.bizplanit.com/free.htm

Here you'll find lots of free information from BizPlanIt, a company that helps people design business plans.

### http://www.businessplans.org

Visit this site to get samples and guidance for creating business plans from PlanWrite.

# E-Commerce

### http://www.alertsite.com

This company offers round-the-clock monitoring for your Web site, notifying you of any slow performance, server problems, or broken links.

### http://www.econgo.com

Visit this site to get a free e-commerce site with a shopping-cart system.

### http://www.freemerchant.com

This site offers free e-commerce sites with a store builder, a secure cart, auction tools, and more goodies.

# Finding Clients

### http://www.ework.com

This site is an exchange for workers and managers with thousands of project listings. It helps match up employers with workers.

### http://www.freeagent.com

Free Agent is a marketplace for consulting and freelance projects.

### http://www.freetimejobs.com

This Web site acts as a marketplace that matches part-time contract workers with employers.

### http://www.freelanceworkexchange.com

Visit Freelance Work Exchange for freelance jobs in art, writing, photography, programming, design, and translation.

### http://www.elance.com

This site is a global marketplace for freelancers in a wide variety of fields.

## http://www.smarterwork.com

A truly international job board for freelancers, SmarterWork.com matches work and workers from over 100 countries.

## http://www.ants.com

Ants.com is a well-designed general-freelancer and contract-worker marketplace.

# Government

## http://www.govspot.com

This directory of government services helps you find the right department for filing complaints, getting forms, and much more.

## http://www.sbaonline.sba.gov

The U.S. Small Business Administration offers lots of advice for the beginning small-business owner.

## http://www.uspto.gov

Visit the U.S. Patent and Trademark Office's Web site, where you can register your logo, your company name and motto, or anything else you want to protect as intellectual property.

# Internet

## http://www.getspeed.com

Find out what high-speed Internet services are available in your area by visiting this site.

# http://www.webhosters.com

This site compares hundreds of Web-hosting services, so you can pick the one that's best for your needs.

# http://www.nua.ie/surveys

Get access to the results of hundreds of surveys about Internet-related topics here.

# http://www.ebot.com

This site searches the Web for software updates, and improves file-downloading by allowing you to pause and restart downloads.

# http://www.pcsupport.com

PCSupport.com helps you clean and optimize your hard disk, recommends updates for applications and drives, scans for viruses, and performs automated online backups.

# http://www.epeople.com/home.jsp

A technical-support site for PCs, EPEOPLE.com will answer your questions by e-mail or live chat.

# Legal

# http://www.egripes.com

Name your own price for the legal resolution of a dispute—kind of like Priceline.com does with airline tickets.

# http://www.lawoffice.com

This site offers lots of articles on all kinds of legal issues such as bankruptcy, incorporation, and zoning.

### http://www.sharktank.com

Post a description of your legal needs on SharkTank.com, and attorneys will send you their credentials and rates.

# Marketing

### http://www.ditto.com

This site offers a large database of photos from all over the Web that you can use in your marketing and advertising.

### http://www.eletter.com

This is a company that creates and sends direct mail affordably. Send them your ads and your mailing list, and they will do the stamping, addressing, and mailing.

### http://www.iprint.com

Create your own business cards, stationery, labels, and promotional items using this company's site; they will print them up and send them to you pronto.

### http://www.seeuthere.com

This company plans events and meetings, handles ticketing, credit-card sales, reminders, and all the other details.

### http://www.thinkdirectmarketing.com

For only a few cents per name, you can get a list of sales prospects from this company, targeted as broadly or as narrowly as you like.

# Online Storage

## http://www.netdrive.com

This site provides 100MB of room for anything you want to put online. Your account appears in Windows just like any other drive.

## http://www.myspace.com

Get 300MB of storage space in exchange for completing a survey; you can get more space by recruiting friends to use the service.

## http://www.zing.com

This site offers unlimited storage for your graphic images and includes a slideshow mode for browsing.

# Organizations

## http://www.hoaa.com

The Home Office Association of America site contains information about how to join and what benefits you'll receive.

## http://www.soho.org

SOHO America is organization that provides business advice and resources to small-office/home-office workers. Some information on the site is free; to access other items, you must first join SOHO America.

# Publications

## http://mags.smalloffice.com/homeofficecomputing/index.htm

This, the online version of *Home Office Computing* magazine, provides selected articles from current and back issues.

## http://www.homeofficemag.com

Visit this site for an online preview of the current issue of *Entrepreneur's Home Office Magazine*.

## http://www.homeofficelife.com

At this site, author and consultant Lisa Kanarek answers questions and offers tips about working from home.

## http://www.gohome.com

*Business @ Home*, an online magazine for people who work from home, is available here.

## http://www.toolkit.cch.com

This site features the CCH Business Owners Toolkit, with links to news stories affecting small business, as well as a SOHO guidebook.

## http://www.entrepreneurmag.com

This site hosts the online version of *Entrepreneur* magazine, with articles and tips for small startup businesses.

## http://www.ivillage.com/work

The Work at Home section of iVillage.com includes a message board, an Experts section, and many articles and tools.

# Reference Library

### http://www.bartleby.com

Bartleby.com offers a free online collection that includes a dictionary, encyclopedia, thesaurus, style guide, and book of quotations.

### http://www.northernlight.com

Use this site to search 62,000 full-text articles from journals and magazines, as well as the Web.

### http://www.refdesk.com

Like a library reference desk, this site can help you find reference information or statistics.

### http://www.uswestdex.com

This site contains a national database of people and businesses. You can also get a list, with maps, of all businesses in a particular city.

### people.yahoo.com

Yahoo! People Search is a free service that helps you find individuals and businesses, either by e-mail address or by mailing address and phone number.

# Shipping

### http://www.simplypostage.com

This site works with a PC-connected postage scale and a printer to help you meter your packages and print postage.

## http://www.smartship.com

SmartShip.com lists the rates and pickup times of all overnight carriers in your area.

## http://www.stamps.com

Visit this site to print postage on your printer, primarily for letters. You weigh them on your own postage scale and enter the weight and destination.

# Shopping

### http://www.formsplanet.com

At FormsPlanet, you can customize and order business forms online.

### http://www.atyouroffice.com

This office-supply store carries over 30,000 products you can order online.

### http://www.officeme.com

This site offers one-stop shopping for the phone services, accounting, marketing, and supplies you need to start a home business.

### http://www.consumersearch.com

Read reviews for a variety of products, including computers and electronics.

### http://www.pricegrabber.com

Compare prices for high-tech items all over the Web.

## http://www.computershopper.com

Compare prices for computer hardware and software at this site.

## http://www.homeofficedirect.com

Buy furniture for home offices at this site.

# Small Business

## http://www.quicken.com/small_business

A subset of the Quicken.com Web site, this area is geared specifically for small business users. The content changes frequently, but there is a wealth of information here.

## http://www.businessknowhow.com

Visit this site to read lots of good articles about general business principles, not necessarily confined to the home office.

# Taxes

## http://www.iaccounting.com

Shop for local accountants in your price range at this site.

## http://www.irs.gov

Access resources for tax preparation at this site, including advice, downloadable forms, and explanations of terms.

## http://www.taxpenalty.com

If you've paid tax penalties in previous years, this site can help you recalculate your payroll and estimated taxes so it won't happen again.

## http://www.1040.com

Download your 1040 forms for the next tax year, and read about breaking tax news and updates at this Web site.

## http://www.smbiz.com

This site contains lots of up-to-date tables and statistics such as federal tax rates and revenue rulings.

## http://www.members.aol.com/bmethven

This Business Law Site offers legal checklists and information about electronic commerce, trademarks, and copyrights.

# Telecommunications

## http://www.decide.com

This site walks you through choosing a cellular phone plan.

## http://www.bell-atl.com/sbs

Bell Atlantic offers small business telephone service information here.

## http://sbc.bus.att.com/small_business

Visit this site for small business telephone information from AT&T.

## http://www.bellsouth.com/bs_atyoubus.html

Bell South's site offers information about business telephone service at this Web site.

## http://www.pacbell.com/Products_Services/WorkAtHome

At this site, Pacific Bell presents information about its work-at-home telephone services and other useful information about home-office telephony.

# Telecommuting

## http://www.gilgordon.com

Here you'll find lots of articles about telecommuting, along with links and other resources for working from home.

## http://www.telecommutemagazine.com

This site hosts an online-only magazine with articles about telecommuting, as well as providing a gateway to Workexchange, an online job board for freelancers.

## http://www.telecommute.org

This is the Web site for the International Telework Association and Council, a non-profit organization for people who telecommute.

# A Concise Guide to Schedule C

If you operate your business in the United States, you must file a federal income tax statement each year. If your business is a sole proprietorship (that is, not incorporated and not a partnership with anyone else), you will include a form called Schedule C, "Profit or Loss from Business (Sole Proprietorship)" with your main tax form (1040).

**NOTE**    Small businesses and statutory employees might be eligible to file a shortened version of Schedule C called C-EZ. Schedule C-EZ contains a subset of the fields described in this appendix. To use C-EZ, you must meet all the following criteria: 1) have expenses of less than $2,500; 2) use the Cash accounting method; 3) not have had an inventory at any time during the year; 4) not have had a net loss; and 5) had only one business as a sole proprietor.

There's a lot more to the average home worker's taxes than just Schedule C. At the minimum, you will also need to fill out form 1040, and probably Schedule A (*Itemized Deductions*), Schedule SE (*Self-Employment Tax*), and Form 8829 (*Expenses for Business Use of Your Home*). Also, if you have capital equipment to depreciate, you'll need Form 4562 (*Depreciation and Amortization*). However, most new business owners find Schedule C especially intimidating at first.

I am not an accountant, and this information should not be construed as financial advice, but I am a small-business owner myself, and I've filled out this form many times. The following lists each box on the form and explains, briefly, what to put in each box. You can also refer to the Sunday afternoon session in the book for more tax help. You can also get instructions for Schedule C from the IRS, either in person, by phone, or at their Web site (http://www.irs.gov).

# Boxes A through H

In this section, you fill in the essential identifying information about yourself and your business.

| Box | Box Title | Comments |
|-----|-----------|----------|
| | Name of Proprietor | |
| | Social Security Number | |
| A | Principal Business or Profession, Including Product or Service | Be specific here. For example, don't just put "appraisal," but rather "Real estate appraisal for lenders." |
| B | Enter Code from Instructions | Enter the code that most closely matches your business type. Look it up online at http://www.irs.gov if you don't have the instructions handy. |
| C | Business Name | If you use your own name as the business name, leave this blank. |
| D | Employer ID Number (EIN), if any | EINs are required only for those who have a Keogh plan or are required to file an employment, excise, estate, trust, or alcohol, tobacco, and firearms return. If you need an EIN, file form SS-4. Leave it blank if you don't have one; do not enter your Social Security number here. |

| Box | Box Title | Comments |
|-----|-----------|----------|
| E | Business Address | Make sure you include a full address, with all the info required for mail to reach you, such as suite number. Use your street address, not a post office box. If your business address is the same as the home address that you entered on the 1040 form, you can leave this blank. |
| F | Accounting Method | Choose your accounting method: cash, accrual, or other. If you choose other, enter the method in the box provided. If you have inventory, you must use the accrual method. If you did not keep formal accounting records, you must use the cash method. |
| G | Did you "Materially Participate" in the Operation of this Business During [*Year*]? | This is almost always Yes for a home-based business. It would be Yes if any of the following were true: 1) You participated in the business for at least 500 hours; 2) You were the only one participating in the business; 3) You |

| Box | Box Title | Comments |
|-----|-----------|----------|
| G | *(continued)* | participated for over 100 hours and you participated at least as much as any other person in it; 4) You participated in all significant business activities for at least 500 hours; 5) You participated for any five of the prior 10 tax years; 6) The activity is a personal service activity in which you participated for any three prior tax years; 7) You participated in a regular, continuous, and substantial basis for more than 100 hours. |

**NOTE** Why is this "material participation" so important? Well, it's primarily an issue if the business is reporting a loss. You can mark the No box if the business was a passive activity; if so, there are limits on the allowable loss you can claim. You must fill out Form 8582 to figure the exact amount.

| Box | Box Title | Comments |
|-----|-----------|----------|
| H | If You Started or Acquired This Business During [*Year*], Check Here | Also mark this box if you are reopening or restarting a business after temporarily closing it, and you did not file a Schedule C or C-EZ for the business last year. |

# Part I: Income

In this section, you enter the income your business made. This can include sales, service fees, royalties for publications, and other forms. Don't attempt to adjust the figures for any expenses at this point; that's done later.

| Box | Box Title | Comments |
| --- | --- | --- |
| 1 | Gross Receipts or Sales Income for the Business. | The total amount of gross. This includes income from 1099 Misc forms you received from customers and income from W-2 forms on which the Statutory Employee checkbox was marked, plus any other receipts. However, if you had both self-employment income (1099-MISC) and statutory employee income (W-2), do not combine the amounts on a single Schedule C; fill out separate forms for each business. |

**NOTE**   Many workers who work solely on commission are classified as statutory workers, including some insurance agents, salespeople, and home workers.

| Box | Box Title | Comments |
|-----|-----------|----------|
| 2 | Returns and Allowances | The amount of money you paid back to customers or vendors who returned what you sold for a refund or who received rebates or cash-back incentives from you. |
| 3 | Subtract Line 2 from Line 1 | |
| 4 | Cost of Good Sold | The amount you paid for any items that you sold. See lines 33 through 42 to calculate this. |
| 5 | Gross Profit. Subtract Line 4 from Line 3 | |
| 6 | Other Income, Including Federal and State Gasoline or Fuel Tax Credit or Refund | Enter any credits you received, if applicable. These can include finance reserve income, scrap sales, bad debts you recovered, interest on accounts receivable, prizes or awards related to the business, and other miscellaneous business income. You might have received a 1099-PATR form reporting some such income. |
| 7 | Gross Income. Add Lines 5 and 6. | This is the amount of profit your business made before expenses are subtracted. |

# Part II: Expenses

In the Expenses section, you offset the gross income from Part I with the money you paid to run the business. This can include travel expenses, office expenses, depreciation of capital equipment, employee salaries, and so on.

| Box | Box Title | Comments |
|---|---|---|
| 8 | Advertising | Enter costs both for generating and for placing ads. |
| 9 | Bad Debts from Sales or Services | If a customer did not pay and you wrote off the debt in your accounting, enter the loss amount here. If you later collect on the debt, you can report it as income on line 6 that year. |
| 10 | Car and Truck Expenses | You can deduct your actual expenses or take the standard mileage rate. If you used your vehicle for hire or used more than one vehicle in the business, you must use actual expenses. There are other rules about which method you must use; see the Schedule C instructions. Actual expenses include maintenance, gas, and payments. You must fill out Part IV of Schedule C if you claim any car or truck expenses. |

| Box | Box Title | Comments |
|-----|-----------|----------|
| 11 | Commissions and Fees | Enter any amounts you paid to others for sales leads, referrals, or other business relationship costs. |
| 12 | Depletion | Home businesses won't have depletion; this refers to depleted natural resources, such as timber. See Publication 535 for details. |
| 13 | Depreciation and Section 179 Expense Deduction | Depreciation is the annual deduction allowed to recover the cost or other basis of business or investment property that has a useful life substantially beyond the tax year. Examples include your business vehicle and your business furniture. Fill out form 4562 to total up your depreciation expense. Section 179 allows you to deduct the full cost of a depreciable item in the year it was purchased, up to a certain amount. Fill out Form 4562 for that. |

**NOTE**   See the Sunday afternoon session for more information about depreciation as it relates to your home office.

| Box | Box Title | Comments |
| --- | --- | --- |
| 14 | Employee Benefit Programs (Other Than on Line 19) | This can include accident and health plans, group term life insurance, and child-care assistance programs. But don't include contributions you made on your own behalf as a self-employed person for accident, health, or life insurance. You can deduct a portion of that expense on Form 1040, line 28. |
| 15 | Insurance (Other Than Health) | Deduct your business-insurance premiums here, such as liability insurance. |
| 16 | Interest | Deduct interest on business loans or on mortgages for property used for the business here. Don't include interest from your primary residence or from interest on investment property. Use line 16a if you received a Form 1098 for the interest, or use line 16b and attach an explanatory statement if you did not. |

**NOTE**    You might not have received a Form 1098 if you share the mortgage with someone else and the Form 1098 comes to that person's tax ID number instead of yours. In that case, include a note with the person's name, address, and tax ID.

| Box | Box Title | Comments |
| --- | --- | --- |
| 17 | Legal & Professional Services | This includes tax advice and any tax-preparation fees. |
| 18 | Office Expense | Cleaning, plant watering, and landscaping are not usually applicable to home offices. |
| 19 | Pension and Profit-Sharing Plans | If you contributed to any pension or profit-sharing plans for your employees, enter them here. This does not include contributions for you; enter those on Form 1040, line 29 instead. |
| 20 | Rent or Lease | In 20a, enter the costs for any vehicles or equipment used in the business. Check the Schedule C instructions to calculate an *inclusion amount* if you leased for a term of 30 days or more. In 20b, enter the rent or lease amount for other business property (for example, if you rented a copier or a computer system). |

| Box | Box Title | Comments |
|---|---|---|
| 21 | Repairs and Maintenance | Include repairs for any business items, but do not include repairs and maintenance for your home; you'll deduct those on Form 8829. |
| 22 | Supplies | Your office supplies (copier paper, printer toner, paperclips, and so on). |

**NOTE** Supplies can be distinguished from capital equipment (subject to depreciation on line 13) by their consumability. If something is used up completely in a single year, it's a supply; otherwise it's capital equipment.

| Box | Box Title | Comments |
|---|---|---|
| 23 | Taxes and Licenses | If you pay a fee or tax for a license to practice your profession or to be certified or bonded, deduct the fee here. |
| 24a | Travel | Your expenses for lodging and transportation connected with overnight travel for business. There are exceptions and limits on foreign travel; see the Schedule C instructions. |

| Box | Box Title | Comments |
|-----|-----------|----------|
| 24b | Meals and Entertainment | Enter your total business meal and entertainment expenses while traveling for business. You can use a standard meal allowance instead of the actual amounts; see Publication 463. There are strict rules for meal or entertainment eligibility; see the Schedule C instructions. |
| 24c | Enter Nondeductible Amount Included on Line 24b | Figure out how much of the amount on line 24b is not deductible, and enter the non-deductible amount here. |
| 24d | Subtract line 24c from line 24b. | |
| 25 | Utilities | Enter utility expenses for the business, but do not include home utility expenses; deduct a portion of them on Form 8829. |
| 26 | Wages (Less Employment Credits) | Enter the total salaries and wages for your employees but not for yourself, minus any credits (such as Work Opportunity Credit, Indian Employment Credit, or Welfare-to-Work Credit). You'll need to fill out separate forms for each type of credit you received, if any. (See the Schedule C instructions.) |

| Box | Box Title | Comments |
|---|---|---|
| 27 | Other Expenses | Enter the total here from line 48 on page 2 (Part V of Schedule C). |
| 28 | Total Expenses | Add up lines 8 through 27. |
| 29 | Tentative Profit (Loss). | Subtract line 28 from line 7. |
| 30 | Expenses for Business Use of Your Home. Attach Form 8829. | Fill out form 8829 to calculate your home-office deduction, and enter the total from that form here. |
| 31 | Net Profit or (Loss). | Subtract line 30 from line 29. If you have a profit, enter it on Form 1040, line 12, and also on Schedule SE, line 2. If you have a loss, see box 32. |
| 32 | If You Have a Loss, Check the Box That Describes Your Investment in This Activity. | The rules at this point get fairly complex; refer to the Schedule C instructions. You must choose between two check boxes: All Investment Is at Risk, or Some Investment Is Not at Risk. |

# Part III: Cost of Goods Sold

In this section you will deduct the amount you spent to buy inventory or to fabricate goods to sell. If you did not have inventory, you can skip this section.

| Box | Box Title | Comments |
|-----|-----------|----------|
| 33 | Method(s) Used to Value Closing Inventory | Choose a checkbox: Cost, Lower of Cost or Market, or Other (Attach Explanation). Normally the value is the cost you paid, but if the items have depreciated since you bought them, you can take the lower amount. |
| 34 | Was There Any Change in Determining Quantities, Costs, or Valuations Between Opening and Closing Inventory? If "Yes," Attach Explanation. | Normally the answer is No. Choose Yes and attach an explanation if you changed the company's inventory calculation system this year. |
| 35 | Inventory at Beginning of Year. If Different from Last Year's Closing Inventory, Attach Explanation. | This is your company's opening inventory value at the beginning of the year. |
| 36 | Purchases Less Cost of Items Withdrawn for Personal Use. | The amount you spent to buy inventory. |
| 37 | Cost of Labor. Do Not Include Any Amounts Paid to Yourself. | Also do not include money paid to employees, which you already deducted on line 26. |

| Box | Box Title | Comments |
|-----|-----------|----------|
| 38 | Materials and Supplies | If you fabricated any products, enter the amount you paid for those raw materials. |
| 39 | Other Costs | Enter any miscellaneous costs associated with your inventory here. |
| 40 | Add Lines 35 through 39 | |
| 41 | Inventory at End of Year | Enter your year-end inventory value. |
| 42 | Cost of Goods Sold | Subtract line 41 from line 40. Enter the result here and also on line 4. |

# Part IV: Information on Your Vehicle

Fill out this section only if you claimed car or truck expenses on line 10 and are not required to file Form 4562 for this business. Refer to the Schedule C instructions for line 13 to determine whether you must use Form 4562.

| Box | Box Title | Comments |
|-----|-----------|----------|
| 43 | When Did You Place Your Vehicle in Service for Business Purposes? (Month, Day, Year) | |

| Box | Box Title | Comments |
|---|---|---|
| 44 | Of the Total Number of Miles You Drove Your Vehicle During [*Year*], Enter the Number of Miles You Used Your Vehicle For | These numbers are important for calculating the number of allowable miles to deduct. Commuter miles are not deductible. |
| a | Business | |
| b | Commuting | |
| c | Other | |
| 45 | Do You (or Your Spouse) Have Another Vehicle Available for Personal Use? | Mark Yes or No. |
| 46 | Was Your Vehicle Available for Use During Off-Duty Hours? | Mark Yes or No. |
| 47a | Do You Have Evidence to Support Your Deduction? | This could include receipts, notations in a log book, or an employer's testimony. |
| 47b | Is the Evidence Written? | Choose Yes if at least some of the evidence is in written or computerized form, as opposed to a person's testimony. |

# Part V: Other Expenses

Use this section to enter other expenses that do not fall neatly into other categories on Schedule C. For example, you might enter the costs of subscriptions to trade publications that you need in order to do your job or the cost of books you bought to do research for a certain client.

Do not include charitable contributions here; these are deducted on Schedule A. Also do not include business equipment or furniture here (that would be line 13 instead) or home-office expenses (record those on Form 8829).

| Box | Box Title | Comments |
|---|---|---|
| 48 | Total Other Expenses | Enter the total here, and then transfer it to line 27 as well. |

# INDEX

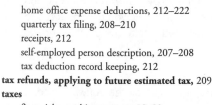

# License Agreement/Notice of Limited Warranty